THE Aftermath OF THE Mexican Revolution

THE **Aftermath** OF THE **Mexican Revolution**

SUSAN PROVOST BELLER

 TWENTY-FIRST CENTURY BOOKS MINNEAPOLIS

To all of my grandchildren, Mike, Samantha, Katrina, Liam and Xavier

Consultant: Zack Cuddy, master's degree in Latin American studies from San Diego State University, San Diego, CA

The image on the jacket and the cover is of Mexican general Pancho Villa riding with his men after the victory at Torreon in 1914. (© Time & Life Pictures/Getty Images)

Twenty-First Century Books
A division of Lerner Publishing Group, Inc.
241 First Avenue North
Minneapolis, MN 55401 U.S.A.

Website address: www.lernerbooks.com

Library of Congress Cataloging-in-Publication Data

Beller, Susan Provost
    The aftermath of the Mexican Revolution / by Susan Provost Beller.
       p.   cm. — (Aftermath of history)
    Includes bibliographical references and index.
    ISBN 978–0–8225–7600–6 (lib. bdg. : alk. paper)
       1. Mexico—History—Revolution, 1910–1920. 2. Mexico—History—Revolution,
    1910–1920—Influence. 3. Mexico—History—20th century. I. Title.
    F1234.B435 2009
    972.08'16—dc22   2007050825

Manufactured in the United States of America
1 2 3 4 5 6 –BP—14 13 12 11 10 09

Contents

Decade of Turmoil

O N THE NIGHT OF February 22, 1913, Francisco Madero, for a short time president of Mexico, rode in a car on the way to exile. It was a terrible end to what had seemed a promising story. Less than a year and a half had passed since he had made himself the hero of Mexico, calling for the people to rise and free themselves from the long dictatorship of Porfirio Díaz. To his surprise, the people had responded to his call. Several regional armies had fought with federal forces to bring the Díaz regime, called the Porfiriato, to an end. Elected in the presidential contest that followed, Madero had assumed office filled with hope that he could make a difference in the lives of the people of Mexico.

But the issues of the day were complex, and his supporters did not give him time to make the needed changes. His friends Emiliano Zapata and Pascal Orozco had taken up arms against him because they felt he had deserted the revolutionary cause. Then the man he had appointed to protect the government had betrayed him. That man, Victoriano Huerta, would be assuming the presidency for himself. Riding with Madero was his vice president, José Maria Pino Díaz. Both men were being transferred from the presidential palace to a nearby prison. There they would await their transport out of the country. What they may have been thinking or talking about has been lost to history, since they never completed that journey.

The car was ambushed, and the two men were killed before they reached the prison. The official story was that they had attempted to escape, but almost no one believed that account. What had begun in 1910 as the removal of a dictator had just crossed the line into civil war and revolution.

THE UNEXPECTED REVOLUTION

Two years before it began, no one would have predicted that Mexico would be torn by a revolution. In 1908 an American reporter, James Creelman, was allowed an extensive personal interview with the longtime

president of Mexico, Porfirio Díaz. In his article, the reporter quoted the American secretary of state Elihu Root, who called Díaz "one of the great men to be held up for the hero-worship of mankind." Root praised Díaz's skills at governing his people and at the modernization he had brought to Mexico. The reporter spoke of the hopes that Mexican economic success raised for other countries in Latin America. Díaz himself had told the reporter, "I can say sincerely that office has not corrupted my political ideals . . . I cannot cease to serve this country while I live."

"Office has not corrupted my political ideals . . .
I cannot cease to serve this country while I live."

—Porfirio Díaz, 1908

How could a country whose leader had been described in such terms in 1908 be wracked by revolution just two years later? How could Porfirio Díaz be described as a great hero one year and the source of Mexico's problems two years later? The issues that brought revolution were already in place in 1908. These issues involved land ownership, the role of the Catholic Church, foreign influences in Mexico's affairs, and the status of the country's many poor and indigenous (native) peoples. Those in power largely ignored these issues. And in the Porfiriato, it was dangerous to discuss problems that the government did not wish to deal with. So they went unsolved for a long time. When efforts finally began to resolve these issues, the result was years of strife in Mexico.

Missing Voices of History

HISTORY, FOR THE MOST PART, has been written by and about important people. The voices of the vast majority of people have been lost. Those people lived and died, and the stories of their lives are gone. The history of Mexico is a history of lost voices. Few primary sources exist from the period of the Mexican Revolution. Those that do come mainly from people with a particular point of view. Although the revolution is a fairly recent event in Mexican history, few written records document the conversations and thinking of those who took part in the revolution.

The overwhelming majority of the Mexican people at the beginning of the revolution were illiterate. Thus they left no written records for history. Many of the leaders of the revolution were assassinated before they could put their thoughts on paper. The first-person accounts that we do have come mostly from foreigners or from news accounts of the time.

There are many accounts of the attack on Columbus, New Mexico, in 1916 by the private army of northern Mexico under the command of Pancho Villa, for example. But these accounts come mostly from Americans who responded to the attack rather than from those who waged it. Historians face a daunting task trying to reconstruct the chaotic story of Mexico's past, well aware of all the missing voices that will never be heard.

Official lists give an even dozen names of Mexican presidents during the period beginning with Porfirio Díaz in 1910 and ending with Álvaro Obregón in 1920. Some served only briefly between changes in leadership. The changes in regimes were violent, usually ending in the assassination of the outgoing president. The sheer number, however, shows that throughout these ten years in Mexico, chaos ruled. Each new president seemed to have answers to the country's many problems. Yet each failed to rally the people and make lasting and effective changes. No president seemed able to satisfy the anger of the people, who wanted fast and fair solutions to the country's problems.

Three years into the revolution, the *New York Times* would write that "Mexican politics are still in the barbarous [savage] stage, and a successful revolutionist in Mexico almost instinctively proceeds to complete his victory by putting to death the rival whom he had defeated." Eventually the decade of turmoil did come to an end. A new constitution was crafted. New leaders began to make the real changes needed to improve the lives of the people of the country.

The aftermath of that revolution can still be felt in the lives of Mexicans in the twenty-first century. The issues that faced Mexico between 1910 and 1920—the issues that led to and fueled revolution—were only partly resolved by the time the revolution had ended. Historians debate the outcome of the revolution. Some wonder if it really changed anything. The changes wrought by revolution are still evolving almost a century after the revolution began. The aftershocks of the revolution can still be felt in Mexico.

CHAPTER 1

Prelude to Revolution

NEWS COVERAGE FROM TWO YEARS BEFORE the outbreak of the 1910 revolution painted a glorious picture of life in Mexico. Yet the problems that caused the revolution were already well established. Anyone willing to look at the situation with a critical eye could see them. However, with Mexico under the firm control of Porfirio Díaz, looking too closely at what was happening was discouraged. But not looking did not solve the problems. And the problems were many. They included the need for land and labor reform and the need to decrease the role of the Catholic Church in politics and education. The country also needed political stability and a reduction of foreign influence in Mexican affairs.

Mexico in the early years of the twentieth century was ripe for a revolution. Even some members of the privileged classes saw the issues and argued for reform. Although Díaz liked to talk about how he encouraged democratic ideals, he usually cut off any discussion of those ideals. And after a while, the problems grew worse.

THE PEONAGE SYSTEM

From the time of the Spanish conquest of Mexico in 1519, ownership of land in Mexico was in the hands of a very small portion of the population. The Spanish conquerors had divided the land into large estates. These estates were given to people who had come from Spain or were descended from Spaniards. These hacendados, as they were

Geography Is Destiny

AT THE TIME OF THE Spanish conquistadors, Spain was not the only European seafaring power trying to build an empire. Great Britain, France, and Portugal were also expanding outward, acquiring territory in far-flung places. They had the resources to build and equip the ships that were needed for exploration and the financial ability to support settlement and conquest.

In the Americas, all four of the major European seafaring powers carved out their own colonies. Where they settled, however, was a matter of luck in where their ships first landed. The geography and resources of the places they settled determined whether the colony was profitable for the mother country.

Mexico's riches lay in minerals and oil. The Spanish conquistadors were given their mission of conquest in order to extract the silver that was thought to be abundant there and to return it to Spain. But silver and gold proved elusive. The Spanish thought they were being tricked out of what was rightly theirs by the indigenous peoples. So they did little to develop the Mexican colony. In the years after independence, the development of those deposits of minerals and oil was seen as a way to make Mexico strong economically. That desire led to the modernization plans of Porfirio Díaz, and ultimately, to the Mexican Revolution.

called, owned the land. They also owned the services of the peoples already living on the haciendas, as the estates were called. Most of these people were native to Mexico. Their families were of Indian descent and had lived in Mexico for centuries. They worked the land for the owners much like the serfs in Europe during medieval times. This system used in Mexico is known as peonage. The workers are known as peons.

Before the hacendados, the peons had lived on the land and had grown their own food. Under the hacendados, they were no longer free to do this. They could continue to grow food for themselves and their families but only if they worked for the landowner and paid him a fee. Under this system, many peons fell deeply into debt. Few could afford the fees, so they added hours to their workday to work off the debt. As a result of this arrangement, most peons had little time for growing or selling their own crops, which meant they could not feed their families or earn money to pay for their other needs.

FAST FACT

MEXICO IS RICH IN NATURAL RESOURCES INCLUDING PETROLEUM, SILVER, COPPER, GOLD, LEAD, ZINC, NATURAL GAS, AND TIMBER.

Like the serfs in medieval Europe, the peons had no hope of ever breaking the cycle of dependence. The result was a form of economic slavery from which the peon could not escape. "Landowners . . . set the parameters of the peons' workaday lives," wrote historian Marjorie Becker. It was a life marked, she further noted, by a "dawn-to-dusk schedule," and with wages that were half what the average worker would need to supply even the most basic food and clothing requirements.

The system did not improve after the Spanish were overthrown and Mexico became independent in 1810. The wealthy hacendados

Serfs and Peons

IN THE MIDDLE AGES (usually dated from the fall of the Roman Empire in the fifth century until the beginning of the Renaissance in the sixteenth century) in Europe, peasants were bound to their lords in a system known as serfdom. Most historians consider this to be a form of slavery. The peasants had no rights, and their labor was forced by the lords of the manors on which they lived. They could own small pieces of property, unlike actual slaves, but they were bound to the land. That meant that when the land was sold, the serfs went with it to the new owner. The vast majority of the property in Europe during the Middle Ages was owned either by wealthy lords, the Catholic Church, or the king.

The system under which Mexico's poor labored before the 1910 revolution is known as peonage. Legally, peonage was a relationship between two free people, one of whom owed the other money. To pay his debt, the peon became bound or indentured to the person to whom he owed money until he had earned enough to pay his debt. The conquered indigenous peoples of Mexico were forced into the system as workers who were entitled to receive a wage. However, the system did not allow them to receive enough money to buy their freedom.

remained in control, and the peons fell further and further behind. By the time of the Porfiriato, the abuses of the peasants under the peonage system threatened to collapse the whole structure of society. Anger was rising among the peons. Open revolt was on the way as they finally responded violently to the years of abuse.

LAND OWNERSHIP

When Díaz assumed the presidency in 1876, he did so with the intention of modernizing Mexico and correcting at least some of the abuses of the peonage system. One area that required modernization involved land ownership records. Records of land ownership were incomplete and contradictory. Organizing the records and establishing who had owned the land and when would not by itself solve the problems of the peons. But Díaz saw it as a much-needed step on the path to modernization. He made it a priority of his presidency to modernize the land records system. Clear land titles (records that establish ownership) would help determine what land had been taken from the peasants without compensation as part of the original land grants by the Spanish. That land could then be restored to the peasants. At least this was Diaz's plan, but the plan was flawed.

The first problem was how the modernization of the land title system was conducted. "Contracts were given to private companies

A PHOTOGRAPH FROM THE 1880s SHOWS A TYPICAL SCENE ON A HACIENDA OF THE TIME PERIOD. A HACIENDA ADMINISTRATOR AND HIS CLERKS, LEFT, CONDUCT BUSINESS WITH A PEON, SEATED ON THE RIGHT, AS OTHER PEONS WAIT THEIR TURN.

to survey the lands . . . for the purpose of discovering the *baldíos,* that is, the lands belonging to the nation. The companies were allowed to retain one-third of all the lands they surveyed," a study by the Brookings Institution (an independent research institution in the United States) concluded. This presented a conflict of interest for the companies. If the land was found to not belong to the owner who claimed it, it reverted to state ownership and the surveyors retained one-third of it for themselves. It was in the best interest of those doing the surveys to declare the land to be public so that they could receive their share. The government acquired land to redistribute to the peons for their own use. But the surveyors earned their one-third of whatever they decided was public, a good return for siding with the government.

The second problem with the system was that the hacendados had the resources to document their claims—sometimes using illegal methods. This meant they were able to keep many of their holdings. It was instead the few indigenous landowners with small holdings and no resources to defend their titles who came out the losers under the land modernization system. "The smaller the landowner, the more likely was his title to be defective," noted the report. "This was particularly true of the Indian villages."

So the means for solving questions of land ownership worked in favor of those who least needed help and against those who were most in need. In fact, the results of the land modernization were disastrous for the peasant class. Within a few years of such surveys, noted the Brookings report, the process "led to the absorption of nearly one-fourth of the total area of the Republic." Instead of broadening the base of land ownership, land was becoming increasingly consolidated into fewer hands. As the project continued over the years of the Porfiriato, the end result, noted the report, was that

Cows pull plows for Mexican farmers working the fields of a large hacienda around 1900.

land in Mexico was "held by proportionately fewer people than at any time in its history."

The hacienda owners as a group actually saw an increase in the size of their holdings under the land modernization system. Some haciendas reached as much as 30 million acres (12.1 million hectares). One historian, P. Edward Haley, noted, "By 1910 nearly half of Mexico belonged to less than three thousand families, while of the 10 million of Mexicans engaged in agriculture more than 9.5 million were virtually without land." The new system had done nothing to improve the lot of Mexico's poor indigenous people.

Unrest among the peasants grew. Revolution came when the inequities of the hacienda peonage system became too great to be lived with any longer. As historian Michael J. Gonzales recorded: "Although Mexicans had fought over land since colonial times, during the Porfiriato the unprecedented convergence of land consolidation, population growth, and inflation in food prices resulted in a groundswell of protest that resulted in revolution." More than any other issue, the problem of land, or agrarian, reform became the rallying cry of the Mexican Revolution.

THE PEONS OF INDUSTRY

Under the Porfiriato, Mexico's economy moved into industrial production. As a result, a new group of workers were needed to fill jobs in industry. Like their rural counterparts, these workers were exploited (taken advantage of) by the small upper class.

Under the Porfiriato, Mexico developed a transportation and communication network that allowed the country to begin to make use of its natural resources, moving away from an economy based only on agriculture. Silver, copper, gold and petroleum were in big demand. Foreign investors and technocrats—the engineers and managers with the knowledge and skills needed to develop these new industries—became an influential voice in government and the economy. But these investors and technocrats were not the ones doing the actual work building the railroads, stringing the telegraph wires, or digging in the mines. That job was done by peasants who moved to the cities in search of better-paying jobs. In many respects, they became the peons of the cities. The industrial workers quickly found themselves sinking deeper and deeper into debt as their low wages proved inadequate to purchase even basic necessities.

What little they did earn was spent at company stores run by their employers. This was not a matter of extravagance or waste on their part. Simply purchasing the most basic of necessities was impossible on the wages that they earned. As their debt grew, they were left with few options to support their families and no way to improve their lot. Like the peons on the haciendas, this new group of working-class Mexicans also felt left behind by the modern Mexico that Díaz was creating.

The worker class involved in industry was not large. One historian puts their numbers at 195,000 out of an entire Mexican population of just under 12 million people. By contrast, Mexico's peasants at the time numbered more than 11 million. As such, they were an

LIKE THE PEONS IN THE COUNTRYSIDE, MEXICAN FACTORY WORKERS WORKED LONG HOURS FOR LOW WAGES. HERE, WORKERS MAKE COFFEE BAGS FROM JUTE AROUND 1903.

almost insignificant proportion of the population that sought change through revolution. However, as a group, the power they could wield through their disruption of the economy was stronger than their numbers would suggest. When General Álvaro Obregón prepared to assume the presidency in 1920, he said (in an interview discussing which were his first priorities upon assuming office) that "One of Mexico's greatest problems at present is that of labor."

THE CHURCH AND ITS POWER IN SOCIETY

Another factor causing unrest in Mexico was the political power of the Catholic Church. The Catholic missionaries (religious workers whose goal was to convert local peoples to Christianity) arrived in Mexico in 1519 with the Spanish *conquistadores* (conquerers). The Spaniards were horrified at what they saw as primitive customs and beliefs. So, although Mexico was conquered for the economic benefits that it could bring to Spain, a major tool in that conquest was the teachings of the missionaries. Historian Matthew A. Redinger explained their role when he wrote, "Catholic missionaries served the *conquistadores* . . . not only in their capacity as evangelizers [converters] of the "heathen" natives but also as agents of royal control of the colony." Religion was used to make the indigenous people serve their Spanish masters. It also made the Catholic Church rich and powerful through its own land ownership and its role in the government of the country.

When Mexico earned its independence from Spain in 1824, it adopted a new constitution that kept the Catholic Church as the state religion of Mexico. This had many implications for the future life of Mexico. Some were political, including requirements that land ownership was reserved for Catholics. Other impacts were ideological, social, and cultural. The Catholic Church, for example, was given

The Barbarians

WHEN THE SPANISH ARRIVED in Mexico in the 1500s, they came as conquerors. They also came to civilize the "barbarians" they found there. Why did they feel the indigenous peoples were barbarians? Mainly it was because the indigenous peoples were not Christian and by definition at the time, non-Christian meant barbarian. However, there was another reason why these people were seen as less than civilized.

The local peoples had their own religious rituals, which revolted and horrified the Spaniards. The peoples of Mexico and Central America had a long history of human sacrifice as part of religious rituals. Recent archaeological findings confirm these practices.

An archaeological dig at the Pyramid of the Moon at Teotihuacán (in the area of modern-day Mexico City) located burial sites that date from almost two thousand years ago. It is thought that these were part of ceremonies to consecrate the temple at various points as it was being built. Animals were also sacrificed, but it is the human finds that illustrate the gruesome nature of these rituals. Victims were frequently buried alive with their hands bound so they could not free themselves.

Europeans also practiced human sacrifice earlier in their own history. The finding of the Lindow man confirms this. His body, located in a bog in northwestern England, shows definite signs of ritualistic killing. Carbon dating suggests the Lindow man lived and died some two thousand years ago and may have been the victim of a ritual practiced by religious leaders known as the Druids. By the time of the Spanish conquest of Mexico, Europeans saw themselves as having moved well beyond such brutality. They felt they owed it to Mexicans to civilize them so that they would give up their barbarian rituals.

the responsibility for all education within Mexico. This responsibility gave the church tremendous influence in determining what people learned about their culture. Religion became a tool for creating a group of citizens who would obey church teachings, as well as serve the needs of the state. The Catholic Church taught that citizenship

WORSHIPPERS GATHER FOR MASS AT A CATHOLIC CHURCH IN MEXICO AROUND 1900. THE CHURCH HAD A GREAT DEAL OF POWER IN MEXICO BEFORE THE REVOLUTION.

meant acceptance of the way in which things were run in Mexico. To question the political order was to defy God.

This was a problem for the indigenous peoples of Mexico. What should have been the voice of the people became instead the means of their oppression. Anyone who might have questioned how they were treated by the government and the hacendados was silenced by the fear of sinning against God.

British observer Ivor Thord-Gray, a supporter of the revolutionary movement who was living in Mexico at the time of the revolution, was disgusted by what he saw in the activities of the Catholic Church.

THE AFTERMATH OF THE MEXICAN REVOLUTION

He wrote of indigenous people being beaten for refusing to convert to Catholicism: "The bull-whip came into play and was freely used." This was an extreme case. The reality was seldom that brutal. Nor did it need to be. These were, for the most part, an uneducated peasantry, quite willing to accept the authority of the church, even as they found themselves "robbed of their land" as Thord-Gray described it.

> *"The bull-whip came into play and was freely used."*
>
> —Ivor Thord-Gray, British resident in Mexico, referring to whippings of local peoples for refusing to convert to Catholicism in the 1800s

Economically the Catholic Church benefited from the system of land ownership and work. The church not only supported the wealthy hacendados. They were hacendados themselves, owning many large haciendas. In fact, the church was one of the wealthiest of all of Mexico's landowners. The peons who worked on church land were not treated any better than other workers. Thord-Gray noted that for the farm worker here, as for those on the privately held plantations (large farms), "his wife and children were pressed into the peonage service 'to pay off the debt.'"

Small groups of liberal thinkers called for more rights for the peasants and the workers. They were secularists, people who believed in the separation of church and state. They were also Protestants, and the Catholic Church saw their crusade as an attempt to lead the people away from the one true religion (Catholicism, in their view). Conflict was building between the secularists and the leaders of the

Catholic Church over what role the church should play in Mexican society. Many of those who encouraged revolution were "violently anticlerical [against the church]. They wished to remove the Church, as a cancerous growth, from the body politic of the Mexican people," in the words of historian Robert Quirk.

THE FAILURES OF MEXICAN EDUCATION

However, it was in the area of education that most believed they could successfully challenge the Catholic Church. The lack of literacy among the peasants after years of Catholic control of education was a problem for the church.

"The Mexicans have never governed themselves," wrote U.S. ambassador Nelson O'Shaughnessy's wife, Edith, to her mother on December 13, 1913, "and there is no reason to suppose they can till a part of the eighty-six per cent that can't read at least learn to spell out a few words." Many people believed that education had to be the first step on the road to establishing a country that served all of the people. They saw the problem the same way Edith O'Shaughnessy did. They saw a population that, under the education of the church, was illiterate and barely surviving.

In 1910, as the revolution began, less than twenty-four percent of Mexican children attended school and at least three-quarters of the population was illiterate. Under the Porfiriato, a small middle class had developed and the wealthy, educated upper class had maintained their numbers. For the lower class, whether living as peons on the large haciendas or toiling in the new industries, education and involvement in civic affairs were not even a possibility. The upper class view was that one educated the peasants to obey and not question the established order. But then they also blamed them for not bettering themselves.

UNDER THE PORFIRIATO, FARMERS LIKE THE MAN SHOWN WITH HIS SON IN THIS LATE NINETEENTH-CENTURY PHOTOGRAPH, WERE NOT PERMITTED AN EDUCATION OR INVOLVEMENT IN COMMUNITY AFFAIRS.

The culture of the country reflected the same level of bias. "Culture" meant glorifying the past of Mexico—the great pre-Columbian empires of the Olmec, Maya, Toltec, and Aztec peoples—while ignoring the needs of their living descendants. Historian Gary MacEoin called it honoring them "only when they are dead," while their descendants "are denied a part in society in every possible way."

The Catholic Church supported the government's policy that educating the indigenous population was not "in their own or the nation's interests," in the words of historian Tomme Clark Call. In doing so, the Church became a target for those wanting revolution.

MEXICO FOR THE MEXICAN PEOPLE

Mexicans, especially indigenous Mexicans, had never had a voice in their political system. The country had lurched from one military

Mexico before the Spanish

AT LEAST THREE SIGNIFICANT cultures existed in Mexico before the arrival of the Spanish. These cultures had a high level of civilization and provide a proud heritage for their modern descendants.

The first such culture were the Olmec, known to archaeologists for the giant sculpted stone heads they created. These heads may have been representations of their kings. They lived around 1200 B.C. in what is now southern Mexico along the coast of the Gulf of Mexico. The Olmec were apparently an agricultural society. Their leaders seem to have been mostly priests, and members of the society engaged in trade and the creation of works of art.

The Mayans, who may have been direct descendants of the Olmec, developed an urban, city-based society by at least A.D. 250. The Mayans were concentrated in two large settlements: one in what is now Guatemala and the other on the Yucatan peninsula in what is now Mexico. The Mayans developed sophisticated religious and astronomical calendars. They also created a written language whose sophistication matches any found in a European culture during this time period. Researchers believe the Mayans merged with other peoples living in the region.

The Aztec culture, which was the dominant culture when the Spanish arrived in Mexico, was an assimilation (mix) of previous Mesoamerican cultures (those of Middle America, the area between North and South America, which included southern Mexico) such as the Maya. Historians believe that their domination of the region began in the twelfth century. The Aztec were excellent engineers, mathematicians, and astronomers. Their culture was sophisticated and complex. Examples of their art, including their impressive Calendar Stone with its representation of the known universe, can be seen at the National Museum of History and Anthropology in Mexico City.

junta (a group of military officers who runs the government after seizing power) to another in the years since gaining independence from Spain, only occasionally having a short period of political stability. In that sense, the presidency of Porfirio Díaz was actually an accomplishment. Díaz had managed to hold on to power for more than thirty years. He brought to Mexico a long period of stability and economic growth.

Beneath the surface of his long reign, however, was a harsh truth. Stability and economic growth had come from the toil of the great majority of Mexicans who had no say in their future. As much as Díaz claimed that Mexico was a democracy, the overwhelming proportion of the population had no experience with democratic rule.

LIVING WELL OFF THE MEXICAN PEOPLE

One group of people who lived well under the Porfiriato were foreign business owners and their managers. "American interests in 1910 held Mexican investments in excess of the total capital owned by the native citizens themselves," wrote historian Haldeen Braddy. If there was one symbolic issue that rankled among the people, it was the Porfiriato's love of foreign business. Taking Mexico back for the Mexicans was an easy rallying point from which to start a revolution.

The story of the Herr family in Cubo, Mexico, is just one example of the numbers of Americans who lived in affluence in the middle of degrading poverty. Robert Woodmansee Herr grew up in a hacienda, closed off from the villagers outside by gates "massive like those of a medieval castle, made of oak four inches (10 centimeters) thick." His palatial home was located in the Mexican village of Cubo, where his father was an American mining engineer. For Robert and his brother, it was a wonderful place to grow up, in a household staffed with a cook, housemaid, laundress, gardener, and handyman.

He and his brother did not play with Mexican children. And his family did not interact with Mexicans who lived in the nearby village. He believed, however, that the Mexicans in the village "were a happy people who accepted their poverty with fatalism and fortitude."

> *"They were a happy people who accepted their poverty with fatalism and fortitude."*
>
> —Robert Woodmansee Herr, 1999, referring to Mexicans in the village of Cubo, where he grew up

Mexico benefited from American business in many ways. Foreigners invested in transportation and communication networks. They also developed mining and petroleum industries. However, few investors were there to help Mexico. They were there because it was profitable for them. "It was a safe land in which to do business. Justice was carried out according to an unwritten, unbreakable law," noted historian Anita Brenner, "the foreigner must be right." Porfirio Díaz actively encouraged foreign businesses to invest in Mexico. He knew that the country did not have the financial resources to develop and modernize without outside help.

Foreign investors, of which the United States and Great Britain were the largest, had the resources required. They developed the industries. They created the transportation needed (mostly railroads) to allow the country to use its natural resources. Foreign businesses earned hefty profits from their investments in oil, silver, copper, gold, lead, zinc, and natural gas.

Historian Robert Quirk referred to this period of the Porfiriato from 1876 to 1910 as a golden age, one in which "The money of foreign capitalists was safe and returned comfortable dividends to those wise enough to buy agricultural lands, oil properties, and mining or railroad stocks." Mexico was receiving the capital (money) needed for development. And foreign investors were reaping great profits. Haley estimated that Americans owned cattle ranches and sugar plantations as well as "three quarters of the mines and more than half the oil fields."

The Mexican economy was prospering for those wealthy enough to be part of it. However, that was quite a small number of the actual population. Herr observed years later that "Mexicans had long watched Americans and other foreigners live among them but above them and on Mexican resources." As Mexico's poor watched those foreigners, they did not see progress. Instead they saw another attempt by the government to keep wealth in the hands of the few.

Díaz's modernization had benefited some people but not the country's poorest and most numerous citizens. Robert Quirk, who had called the years of the Porfiriato a golden age, admitted that during this time "real wages were lower than they had been a century earlier under Spanish rule."

FAST FACT

IN THE THIRTY YEARS BEFORE THE REVOLUTION BEGAN, HISTORIANS SAY, FOREIGN INVESTORS SPENT MORE THAN $1 BILLION CREATING BUSINESSES AND IMPROVING TRANSPORTATION AND COMMUNICATIONS IN MEXICO.

ON THE EVE OF REVOLUTION

All of these problems were simmering beneath the surface of Mexico's new modern image. Díaz felt that he had achieved marvelous things for Mexico. He appeared to truly care for his people and felt that he knew what could best serve their needs. He also felt that the people were not ready to take part in a democracy. But many Mexicans disagreed. They felt that it was time to control their own futures. These different points of view guaranteed that the transition away from Díaz's government would not be peaceful.

CHAPTER 2

Revolution

THE UPHEAVAL THAT BEGAN IN MEXICO IN 1910 is known as the Mexican Revolution. But it was not a revolution in the usual sense of the word. A series of major battles between two armies did not take place. There was no final, well-defined victory. No one signed a treaty that marked the end of the fighting and the beginning of a period of peace. This revolution was marked by political chaos and shifting alliances among ever-changing players. Armies fought each other but not for a single cause or nation. They fought on behalf of generals and other leaders who formed their own armies for their own ends. Each victory brought the overthrow of the government, leading to many new leaders. When a new leader did not quickly meet the demands of those who had placed him in power, he was overthrown. And the next leader, brought to power by a different group of allies, would take his turn at Mexico's helm.

Part of the chaos resulted from lack of agreement about what needed to be accomplished. Armies joined together to put one president in power and then shifted alliances when that president fell out favor. The only common goal among the revolutionary groups was a belief in the need for change. Revolutionaries agreed that agrarian reform was needed. They agreed that the existing elites—whether hacendados, foreign investors, or church leaders—should not be allowed to control Mexico. Revolutionaries believed that a system had to be put into place that would ensure the rights of the peasants and workers of Mexico. They believed that the indigenous peoples were entitled to education and full citizenship.

But they could not agree on how to achieve these goals. Each leader and each group thought it had the answers to Mexico's many problems. But none proved workable or offered lasting solutions. This led to the long period of unrest and instability known as the Mexican Revolution.

THE UPHEAVAL BEGINS

In 1910 the Mexican people faced a presidential election. Most believed that the election would be a sham. They believed that Díaz would be reelected. He had only one opponent—Francisco I. Madero. Madero did not support radical change. He came from a wealthy family. He had conservative views on most issues. However, he believed that the modernization policies of Díaz were moving too quickly. He saw unrest among the peasants and wanted to ease it before trouble came. He wanted to slow down the speed of change in Mexico. He felt that the needs of the peasants had to be taken care of. If not, he feared they would revolt. A revolt would be very

FRANCISCO MADERO, BELOW, RAN FOR PRESIDENT AGAINST PORFIRIO DÍAZ IN 1910. DÍAZ TRIED TO CONTROL THE ELECTION BY IMPRISONING MADERO. THIS PORTRAIT IN OIL WAS PAINTED BY AN UNKNOWN ARTIST BETWEEN 1911 AND 1913.

bad for the country and the large landowners. Representing a group of young, ambitious men who wanted the Porfiriato to end and who organized themselves as the Anti-Reelectionist Party, Madero opposed Díaz for election. Díaz had at first welcomed open debate but soon felt threatened as Madero began to gain supporters. His solution was to imprison Madero.

The president won reelection on June 26, 1910, by an overwhelming number of votes. The margin was so large (many historians say close to 99 percent of the vote) that many Mexicans felt sure he had used some sort of illegal means to win. Madero remained imprisoned until escaping in October. The story is told that the escape was quite easy as he was allowed to go for daily horseback rides with a guard. He simply galloped away from his guard one day while out riding. He fled to the United States. Once there, he issued a declaration, known as the Plan of San Luis Potosi. In it, he declared that Porfirio Díaz "has succeeded in annihilating [destroying] all independent elements, so that it was not possible to organize any sort of movement to take from him the power of which he made such bad use." Madero declared the election to be a fraud and himself to be the rightful president. Then on November 20, 1910, he called for the overthrow of the government of Porfirio Díaz.

The Mexican people responded to Francisco Madero's call for change. In the countryside and in the cities, the common people rose up. They attacked the landowners and people running the country's industries. But this was not an organized revolt.

Revolutionary Legends

THE TWO MOST FAMOUS men of the Mexican Revolution never became presidents of Mexico. But their names have become legends to the people of the country. Leading armies from different parts of the country, representing different groups who needed different results from the revolution, their leadership methods and strategies were strikingly different in every way.

Emiliano Zapata came to the revolution to right a wrong. He represented the peasants toiling in the countryside. He had, from the very beginning, a specific plan in mind to save them—the immediate redistribution of one-third of the land held in haciendas. He remained focused on that one goal of land redistribution all through the revolution and turned away from any leader who would not make immediate agrarian reform the number-one priority. Zapata's army, the Zapatistas, was made up of peasants. They fought in small groups, did not dress in uniforms, and quickly faded back to safety in the countryside. Ultimately, in terms of the results they achieved, they were the most powerful force in the decade of turmoil. It was Zapata's plan, as written in the Plan of Ayala, that became the basis for agrarian reform in the 1917 constitution.

The name of Pancho Villa is forever associated with stories of reckless bravery and romantic crusades that earned him the nickname the Mexican Robin Hood. His was an army without a specific program for change, but with a strong zeal to upend the status quo. His uniformed army traveled as a large group with their families in tow and focused on disrupting railroads, and thus the industrial economy of Mexico. His army absorbed people displaced from communities in the area. He proclaimed himself military governor of the northern state of Chihuahua. When money ran out, he had more printed. He authorized his people to take whatever they wanted. A larger-than-life character, Villa is seen by some as the symbol of the anarchy of the decade of revolution. As he led his followers from adventure to adventure, within changing alliances that even involved attacking the United States, which had been his supporter, he cut a figure of macho hero and became a legend.

It was a spontaneous upheaval by people who wanted change and thought that Madero could bring it. Historian Peter V. N. Henderson called it "a popular uprising without ideology or national leadership."

Díaz had been brought down by a coalition (group) of armies led by regional leaders. They were the ones who had responded to Madero's call for the overthrow of the Porfiriato. The most important of these were the Zapatistas—led by Emiliano Zapata—and the Villistas, led by Doroteo Arango, known as Francisco "Pancho" Villa. Smaller groups had also supported him in his overthrow of the Porfiriato. But these groups disagreed on what needed to be done first. They had different ideas on the pace for enacting the needed reforms. Should land simply be seized from the landowners and given to individual peasants? Should there be a gradual transfer of ownership to allow the peasantry time to acquire the skills and materials they would need to achieve success as individual landowners? Should foreigners be evicted from the country? If so, how would the untrained Mexicans be able to keep mining and other industries functioning?

> *"The Mexican people began fighting because they had to fight to live, and not because they wished to fight."*
>
> —Francisco Madero, 1911

Madero was surprised at the reaction to his call for revolution. He was quick to take advantage of the momentum all the protests generated, however. Speaking with *New York Times* reporter Edward Marshall in May

1911, he described public discontent, rather than his own comments, as the spark that prompted the revolt. He told the reporter that "the Mexican people began fighting because they had to fight to live, and not because they wished to fight. They were intolerably oppressed." This period of unrest continued until May 17, 1911, when the Treaty of Ciudad Juárez brought the resignation of Díaz and peace to the country.

It did not, however, bring Madero to office as president. Madero insisted that the revolt was not about his political ambitions. He recommended that the country have a fair and open presidential election. Madero appointed Francisco León de la Barra to serve as president until the people elected their new leader. The appointment was a mistake. De la Barra was known as a peacemaker, but he was also very conservative. He believed that order must be restored before broader changes could take place. This thinking "ran headlong into the unarticulated [unspoken] objectives of the rural peoples," wrote Henderson. De la Barra was seen as too sympathetic to the old guard leadership from the Porfiriato. People interpreted his failure to make changes to a desire to return to the policies of the Porfiriato.

MADERO AND HUERTA

On November 6, 1911, Madero won election as president. His election was well received. Calm returned to Mexico as people awaited the promised changes. Almost a year had passed since the beginning of the revolution, but so far nothing had been done about the issues of agrarian reform, the need for fair labor practices, the power of foreign interests, and the other forces that had led to the revolt.

A British citizen in Mexico during this time, Ivor Thord-Gray, called Madero "inspired by well-meaning philosophical ideas" but

FRANCISCO MADERO, STANDING IN THE CAR WITH HIS HAT RAISED, GREETS SUPPORTERS AFTER RETURNING FROM EXILE IN THE UNITED STATES IN 1911. MADERO BECAME PRESIDENT OF MEXICO LATER THAT SAME YEAR.

lacking in "experience and common sense." It was one thing to call for revolution, but another to actually govern Mexico and work to solve the issues facing the Mexican people. What was required was strong, firm leadership. Instead, as another historian noted, Madero "oscillated [went back and forth] between conservative and revolutionary forces" and "did not recognize the urgency for satisfying the demands of the revolution."

Madero did not get the time to work out a program to satisfy the needs of his supporters. Increasing dissatisfaction with the pace of change led others to plan their own revolts. Pascual Orozco, a former friend of Madero, broke with him and formed his own army, called the Colorados, or Red Flaggers. Zapata, refusing to work with Madero, announced his own plan calling for immediate return of the land to the peasants. Zapata's Plan of Ayala was intended to reaffirm the revolutionary goals that he felt were being ignored. President Madero "argued that the land problem was a complicated one, that time must be taken to study the matter, that immediate action was impossible." Zapata did not agree and felt that Madero had betrayed the revolution once he became president. Zapata called for the land that had been taken to be immediately restored to the villages, and for the people to take it back if it was not given to them. He called for the overthrow of Madero by armed force if necessary. Madero

PASCUAL OROZCO, CENTER, STANDS WITH MEMBERS OF HIS ARMY, KNOWN AS THE COLORADOS. OROZCO AND THE COLORADOS OPPOSED MADERO. THIS PHOTOGRAPH WAS TAKEN AROUND 1911.

had appointed Victoriano Huerta as commander of the federal army. Huerta defeated the army of Orozco and then joined a conspiracy to overthrow Madero.

In February 1913, fighting broke out in Mexico City, the beginning of *La Decena Trágica,* or The Ten Tragic Days. General Huerta convinced Madero to allow him to bring government troops into the city to protect the capital. It was a ruse and resulted in a coup d'état (an overthrow of the government by the military). Only fifteen months after being elected president, Madero was forced to resign his office by the man he had trusted to lead the army. What had begun as a spontaneous revolt against one president had turned into a revolving door. One president after another tried to address Mexico's problems. And one president after another lost his position after failing to achieve immediate success.

"The dynasties have a way of telescoping in these climes [climates]."

—Edith O'Shaughnessy, wife of the American ambassador to Mexico, 1913

Edith O'Shaughnessy, the wife of the American ambassador, captured the spirit of the times in a letter home to her mother in 1913. "When we arrived in Mexico, beautiful Doña Carmen Diaz was presiding; then came Señora de la Barra, newly married, sweet-faced, and smiling; followed by Señora Madero, earnest, pious, passionate. Now Señora Huerta is the 'first lady'—all in two years

THE AFTERMATH OF THE MEXICAN REVOLUTION

and a half. The dynasties have a way of telescoping in these climes [climates]."

This coup d'état brought Huerta the presidency. On February 19, 1913, the *New York Times* reported that Madero had been deposed and was under house arrest in the presidential palace. The *Times* quoted Huerta's speech from the balcony of that palace, saying that he acted for the good of the country and "had no personal ambitions." Several days later, when Madero was assassinated, Huerta was accused of arranging the removal of his predecessor. It was not a good start for his presidency.

Huerta's priority was to restore order to Mexico. He had difficulty doing this. His term was marked by regional uprisings, most of them brief but bloody. In northern Mexico, in the town of Matamoros on June 4, 1913, for example, a group of rebels captured a small fort controlled by government forces. The defenders were young and inexperienced. The rebels, on the other hand, had gained some experience in the past several years. Most of the townspeople fled across the border into the United States. A few organized as a volunteer regiment to help

VICTORIANO HUERTA, PICTURED HERE IN 1915, BECAME PRESIDENT OF MEXICO THROUGH A COUP D'ÉTAT. HE RESIGNED FROM OFFICE AFTER SEVENTEEN MONTHS.

defend their homes. The rebel forces quickly routed the defenders. More than one hundred people were killed. A photographer who happened to be in Matamoros captured the chilling scene as thirty of those taken prisoner were executed.

Not all uprisings ended this way. Many were brutally suppressed by government forces as Huerta struggled to restore order. During his time in office, he earned the nickname *El Chacal*, or the Jackal, for the harshness of his rule. His return to the conservative policies of the Porfiriato angered the revolutionaries. The Zapatistas pressured Huerta to begin giving land back to the peasants. Huerta's emphasis on restoring order before allowing any reforms to take place and the harshness of his policies brought about his downfall. The various revolutionary groups united, fearing a return to the Porfiriato.

On July 15, 1914, just seventeen months after taking office, Huerta resigned. In his letter of resignation, he claimed that the U.S. government was partly to blame for the loss of his job. In that letter, he acknowledged "the immense difficulties which my Government has encountered" but also spoke of the "protection which a great power [the United States] of this continent had afforded to the rebels."

Though the rebels had united to remove Huerta from power, they could not maintain a united front. Historian Howard F. Cline noted that "The disorder was compounded when these leaders [who overthrew Huerta] of the revitalized Revolution could reach no accord . . . and then battled among themselves for control."

The result was all-out civil war. Regional armies fought each other, trying to place their leaders in the president's chair. The economy was in shambles. Foreign investors had fled to safety in the United States, bringing industrial production to a halt. Workers refused to do their jobs on the haciendas and people were going hungry. What was needed was a political leader who could unite the revolutionaries.

Pancho Villa, seated center, and Emiliano Zapata, seated immediately to Villa's left, are shown with their fellow revolutionaries in 1915. Villa and Zapata both felt that Venustiano Carranza's reforms did not go far enough.

That leader appeared to be Venustiano Carranza, who had served in the government of Madero and been an active participant in the revolts against Huerta. However, he could not come to power without defeating other regional revolutionary leaders such as Pancho Villa and Emiliano Zapata. Both felt Carranza's reform ideas did not go far enough. His own army, known as the Carrancistas, took on the supporters of more radical and immediate reform. It was pressure from the United States under President Woodrow Wilson that finally forced the other groups to support Carranza and create political peace in Mexico.

AMERICAN INTERVENTION

But Carranza was unable to bring order to Mexico once in office. Like presidents before him, he moved too slowly toward reform. This angered those groups that had reluctantly agreed to support his presidency. One of these supporters, Pancho Villa, turned against him. Villa decided that creating more turmoil would force the United States to install another government.

Historian John S. D. Eisenhower called Villa "a man of penetrating intelligence who, had he possessed any degree of self-restraint, might have become one of Mexico's greatest leaders." While fighting in support of Carranza, Villa had captured a Mexican government stronghold at Zacatecas. The loss led directly to the overthrow of Huerta when the federal forces were not able to hold the city. Acting as a bandit, Villa and his cavalry (soldiers on horseback) disrupted government services, robbed trains, and printed their own money, all in an effort to undermine the government.

Villa was attempting to use those same techniques to overthrow Carranza who had been in office since August 1914. U.S. president Woodrow Wilson wanted the revolution over. He saw American interests best served by continuing to support Carranza. Villa disagreed and sent a force of his troops across the border on March 9, 1916, to attack the town of Columbus, New Mexico. It was not a successful attack. Major Frank Tompkins of the 13th U.S. Cavalry recalled that "the Mexicans were poor shots. . . . One of them fired at me with a rifle. . . . He missed me even though he was so close that I easily killed him with a revolver and I was never noted for my excellence in pistol practice."

The Alamo

THE MILITARY INTERVENTION of the United States in Mexico did not begin with the Mexican Revolution. In the 1820s, American citizens began moving to Mexico, receiving grants of land in the province of Tejas, or Texas, which adjoined U.S. territory. In doing so, they accepted the provisions of the 1824 Mexican Constitution. When General Santa Anna became president of Mexico in 1835, he overrode the provisions of the constitution. In the resulting dispute, the settlers of Texas decided to secede (withdraw) from Mexico, considering themselves no longer bound since the constitution was not being followed by the Mexican government.

Santa Anna led a force into the province of Texas early in 1836 to subdue the rebellion. A small group of the Texians, as they called themselves, barricaded themselves in the mission church of San Antonio de Béxar, known as the Alamo, and prepared to meet the attack. Among the defenders were some famous American frontiersmen, including Jim Bowie and David Crockett. Lieutenant Colonel William Barret Travis, in charge of the defense of the mission, refused to abandon the fort to the large advancing Mexican army.

Santa Anna's army began a thirteen-day siege of the fort, which ended with a dawn attack on March 6, 1836, in which all of the Texian defenders were slaughtered within less than an hour. Texas had already declared independence four days prior to the attack, though the defenders never knew that. The outrage from the severity of that attack, and a massacre of Texian forces who had surrendered at Goliad (about 91 miles/146 km away) on March 27, inflamed the American public. Less than a month later, on April 21, a Texian army, although greatly outnumbered, won a crushing victory over Santa Anna's army at San Jacinto (about 225 miles/362 km from the Alamo).

Texas independence was then assured, but securing that independence would take another ten years and a war between the United States and Mexico to finally complete the process. By the time the Treaty of Guadalupe Hidalgo was signed in 1848, ending the Mexican-American War, Mexico had lost one-third of her land area to the United States.

President Wilson responded immediately to the attack, sending troops under the command of General John J. Pershing to Mexico to capture Villa. This Punitive Expedition, as it was called, lasted from March 1916 until February 1917. They never located Villa. But they had several skirmishes with some of his Villistas and on at least one occasion with members of the Mexican army. With U.S. interests more concerned with what was happening in Europe on the Western Front during World War I (1914–1918), the American forces were withdrawn from Mexico.

AN END TO REVOLUTION

Carranza, hoping to meet the demands for change, called for a constitutional convention in September 1916. He did not intend to propose a new constitution. Instead, he wanted to adapt the existing constitution, which had been adopted in 1857. But others saw a constitutional convention as a chance to adopt a new constitution that would affirm the demands of the revolution. And this, they hoped, would end the unrest and bring peace and stability to Mexico.

CHAPTER 3

The Aftermath: A New Day for Mexico

I N THE AFTERMATH OF THE REVOLUTION, Carranza convened the constitutional convention, known as the Querétaro Convention. Delegates met for two months, from November 30, 1916, to January 31, 1917. The 220 delegates included lawyers, military officers, doctors, merchants, miners, and railroad workers. Delegates had to be at least twenty-five years of age, and the majority of them were in their thirties and forties. Most had no governmental experience and were not familiar with the law or the process of writing a constitution.

There were two major points of view among the delegates. One group supported Carranza's position that a new constitution was not needed. Like Carranza, that group felt that the constitution of 1857 should be amended to give the executive (the president) the power to make whatever changes were needed. As a result, the president could control the pace of change. The other group wanted a new

VENUSTIANO CARRANZA IS SHOWN WORKING AT THE PRESIDENTIAL
DESK IN THE NATIONAL PALACE IN 1914. CARRANZA WANTED TO
CHANGE THE CONSTITUTION OF 1857 TO GIVE THE PRESIDENT OF
MEXICO GREATER POWERS.

constitution. They believed the new document should list all changes
to be made, which would mean that they could not be postponed.
Once in the constitution, the changes would become law.

Neither of these groups wanted to return to life as it was before
the revolution. Both had the same goals. Their differences of opinion
were about timing and the extent of the changes to be made immediately. The first group wanted gradual change. The second wanted

immediate change. Historian E. V. Niemeyer Jr. makes the point that "disagreement between the two factions was more of degree than of substance. Both groups were highly nationalistic. They gave no thought to personal gain."

Despite the similarity of goals, "The Querétaro Convention was not a harmonious gathering," said one analyst. This is not surprising for a country that had been engaged in civil war for seven years. Those who were seated as delegates were, for the most part, moderates. The more radical elements of the revolution, such as the Villistas and Zapatistas, were not present at the convention. However, their views were presented to the delegates. And disagreements continued regarding the pace and scope of change.

President Carranza participated in the convention but did not try to control it. He made his views known and explained why he held those views. But he allowed the delegates to work out the decisions on their own and did not interfere with the democratic process.

The United States closely watched the proceedings. As the convention neared its end, a leaked draft of the constitutional document resulted in an official protest from the United States. Secretary of State Robert Lansing sent a protest to the Mexican government about several issues that concerned the American

FAST FACT

THE MEXICAN PEOPLE CELEBRATE THEIR CONSTITUTION EVERY YEAR WITH A NATIONAL HOLIDAY ON FEBRUARY 5. THEY ALSO CELEBRATE THE BEGINNING OF THE REVOLUTION WITH A HOLIDAY ON NOVEMBER 20, TO MARK MEXICAN REVOLUTION DAY.

government. The United States was opposed to a proposal that said foreign industries would have to pay taxes on their properties in Mexico. The United States also felt that a proposal "dealing with the expulsion of obnoxious foreigners . . . without recourse [a path] to appeal" was a problem. Such a policy was "not in accord with the usual practice of nations."

Finally, on February 5, 1917, Carranza signed into law Mexico's new constitution. The constitution had been approved by the convention delegates several days earlier on January 31, 1917. Historian Niemeyer attributes the results of the convention to an outbreak of what he calls "the 'more revolutionary than thou' syndrome" which he felt led the delegates into creating great change because they wanted to prove their revolutionary zeal.

The Old Constitution of 1824

THE 1917 CONSTITUTION was not the first that Mexico had. It was actually the fourth. After Mexico won its independence from Spain in 1821, there was a short period of time when the country was governed by an emperor, Agustín de Iturbide, a former Spanish general. A few years later, his government was overthrown and a constitution was written.

Proclaimed on October 4, the 1824 constitution set up a two-house legislature with a chamber of deputies and a senate, an executive office with an elected president and vice president, and a judiciary with a supreme court of justice. It also mandated Catholicism as the official state religion.

On paper it was an excellent constitution. However, in practice, the presidency was often awarded to the strongest military leader. For example, General Santa Anna became president eleven separate times between 1833 and 1855.

A new constitution in 1857 also did not give the Mexican government the stability it needed. Although it listed the rights of all the peoples of Mexico and provided for a strong legislature that would control the power of the president, it was never effective at protecting the common people. Revolution would have to come before a constitution could be written that would actually be implemented.

The new constitution was a comprehensive social document. "It was the ideas of the Zapatistas and Villistas . . . ," noted historian Larry D. Hill, "that emerged in the constitution." It established citizen rights and abolished slavery. It defined the nation as a pluriculture, meaning it recognized that Mexico was made up of many peoples, and acknowledged the role of the indigenous peoples in Mexican society. It separated the functions of church and state and took from the Catholic Church the civil duties that it had exercised in the past, including responsibility for education. It gave new rights to industrial laborers, including the right to strike. It limited working hours and required a mandatory day off in every week. It mandated extensive agrarian reforms, essentially requiring the government to abolish the large haciendas. The constitution also removed from foreigners those rights of ownership and use of natural resources that had been granted to them over the years. Every one of the issues raised by the revolution was addressed in the new constitution.

THE CONSTITUTION THAT CHANGED EVERYTHING

The new constitution, as written, changed every aspect of life in Mexico. The Mexican people had created a document that took their years of revolution and made their demands the law of their land. No one living in Mexico would ever be the same again.

If you were a wealthy landowner, before the new constitution you were seen to own the workers on your land. From the days of the conquistadors that had been true. You could pay your workers wages that did not allow them to survive without fear of government intervention to protect their interests. Your decisions on how to treat your peons were dependent only on what brought you the best economic benefit. When you awoke on February 5, 1917, all of those assumptions of your power in society were now untrue. The government

Amazing Maize

ONE OF THE MOST PROMINENT crops grown in Mexico is one which was developed by the ancestors of the indigenous peoples of Mexico. The most abundantly produced grain in the world did not come from the area in the Middle East where early humans first domesticated animals and crops. Maize, or corn, was domesticated in Mesoamerica, an area that includes the southern half of Mexico. Geneticists can prove that it was grown in Oaxaca, Mexico, at least nine thousand years ago. Maize was the primary staple in the diet of the peoples living in Mesoamerica, North and South America, and on the islands of the Caribbean before the arrival of Columbus in 1492.

The Mexican people can take credit for domesticating a grain that may become an even more valuable crop in coming years because of its growing use as a reusable energy source. No longer used just for food for humans and feed for animals, corn is a key ingredient in the production of ethanol fuel. Ethanol fuel can be used to run cars and machinery. It can be blended with gasoline as an additive. Over time, engines will be produced that can use it alone as a fuel source. Simple maize has moved from a staple for an agriculturally based indigenous people to possibly part of the solution to the world's energy crisis.

was going to restore to the peasantry the land that had been taken from them and give them power to choose their own destinies. And that land and power would come from what you owned.

If you were a foreign investor who had been developing mining and oil industries in Mexico for the past thirty years, on February 4, 1917, you knew that your word was law. You could maintain unsafe workplace conditions in the name of profit. You could live handsomely while your workers barely eked out an existence in the company towns far from the view of your castle-like hacienda. If there was a dispute between you and your workers, they automatically lost because the government would always assume you were right. On February 5, 1917, your world disappeared. Not only were you now responsible for treating your workers carefully and giving them a living wage, you also were on notice under Article 27 that the government might at any time decide to take over your properties

MEXICAN POLICE ARREST A PRIEST AS PART OF THE GOVERNMENT'S 1917 CRACKDOWN ON THE CATHOLIC CHURCH. THIS PAINTING BY AN UNIDENTIFIED ARTIST IS FROM THAT TIME PERIOD.

and send you home. Article 33 explicitly told you that you had no political role in Mexico.

If you were a member of the Catholic hierarchy, before the new constitution you had unlimited power in Mexico over the religious and educational lives of the people of Mexico. You owned large tracts of land and worked your peons as hard as did the hacendados whose goal was profit. You controlled all education in the country, deciding what topics and how much (or more likely how little) education the peasantry should receive. Under the new constitution, you lost your lands. Article 3 took away your control of education, and you even were restricted in how you ran the church itself in Mexico. This new constitution thoroughly secularized Mexico and brought your influence, which dated from the arrival of the conquistadors, to an end.

If you were a laborer on February 4, 1917, you were subject to the demands and decisions of your employer. You did not have any right to demand either better working conditions or a living wage. Attempts that you might make to do so would be immediately stopped, and you faced being fired or being brutally treated. You found yourself working for such low wages that you could not support yourself and your family. Your only place to buy goods and supplies was probably at a company store where the high prices guaranteed that you would get deeper and deeper in debt to your employer. Article 123 of the new constitution guaranteed the right to work to better your conditions without fear of reprisal. It granted you an eight-hour workday and safer working conditions. More important, the constitution in Article 3 also granted you and your children the right to an education and, with it, the chance to perhaps break free from the cycle of poverty in which your family was trapped.

If you were a peasant toiling on the haciendas before the new constitution, you also had no rights. You were underpaid, overworked,

To Celebrate Diversity

ONE OF THE KEY ELEMENTS of the new constitution of 1917 was recognition of the diversity of the Mexican people. Mexico faced a task of integrating an unusually large number of different ethnic groups into one culture. Even in the twenty-first century, some sixty separate indigenous languages are accepted as official languages by the government. Census figures indicate that 13 percent of the population (about 12 million people) is descended from indigenous peoples. Some sources say that the number of people who place themselves in that group may be as high as 30 percent.

At the time of the 1910 revolution, the indigenous peoples of Mexico were overwhelmingly rural peasants. From an estimated 18 million persons when the Spanish first arrived, their numbers had dwindled to around 2 million sixty years later, mostly through death from disease. The years after Mexican independence did not improve their situation, even though some individuals, such as Benito Juárez, a Zapotec Amerindian who became president of Mexico in the mid-1800s, rose to national prominence. However, the majority of indigenous Mexican peoples worked on farms owned by wealthy Spanish descendants.

The revolution marked an important change for Mexico's indigenous population. For the first time, they were formally acknowledged as part of Mexican society. Their cultures were recognized as part of the national identity that this new Mexico wanted to forge.

and sinking further and further into debt. You had no access to education and no prospect of ever breaking free of the prison of your life. The new constitution said this was wrong. Article 27 said that the land that was taken from you should be returned to you. It said that villages should be given enough land to become self-sustaining. Article 3 also offered you the hope to improve your life and that of your children through education.

If you were one of the indigenous peoples before the new constitution, you had no rights at all. Your culture and language had been removed from you by the conquistadors. You and your labor had been deeded to the large landowners along with the land itself. Mexico before the constitution paid lip service to the glory of your ancient ancestors, the Aztec, the Maya, the Olmec, and the Toltec, but it was believed that all the glory of your people lay in that distant past. You were seen as unable to be educated to a level where you could reclaim that past heritage. The new constitution recognized you as a valued member of Mexican society. It said that your language, your culture, and your heritage was part of the Mexican experience and needed to be incorporated into it. It said that you needed to become a fully participating member of Mexican society. The country, for the first time, wanted to hear your voice.

THE POLITICAL REALITY OF THE NEW CONSTITUTION

In the aftermath of the revolution, the new constitution cemented the demands of the revolutionaries. It mandated agrarian reform, limits on the role of foreigners in the Mexican economy, limits on military involvement in the civilian government of the country, limits on the role of the Catholic Church in governing the country, and increased political and educational access for the poor of Mexico. The president of the constitutional convention, Luis Manuel Rojas, expressed pride in what had been accomplished. He stated that the convention had one goal, "to better the condition of the popular classes, which had always been oppressed." He felt that the convention had met that goal even though there might be "defects" in the document.

Venustiano Carranza became the first president to serve under the new constitution. The constitution mandated that presidents could only serve one term in office. That term would last four years.

The start date of Carranza's term was officially recorded as December 1, 1916. That meant he had four years to begin making the changes set out in the constitution. He found that process difficult, however. Although Carranza had signed the constitution, he had little enthusiasm for it. He felt it did not give him flexibility to make changes at a gradual pace. Despite his opposition to the scope and pace of changes required, he proposed new laws that would allow enactment of the constitution. But he did not carry out these laws as quickly as some wanted. Carranza suppressed the attempts of labor unions to make use of their new rights under the constitution. He was also slow in setting up the machinery for agrarian reform. Historian James D. Cockcroft noted that Carranza "systematically violated the Constitution as President."

Over the next several years, progress was so slow that many of Carranza's supporters felt that he had let them down. He had taken on a job that was inherently difficult. Any president in this position might have been unpopular. Carranza's popularity suffered, both with the winners who wanted the constitution implemented overnight, and with the losers, who wanted to see changes enacted more slowly.

The constitution adopted in the aftermath of the revolution had hurt many people. It especially threatened the power and way of life of wealthy landowners and foreign business interests. Carranza felt pressure from the economic interests such as the hacendados and the foreign business owners. The United States government had supported Carranza, believing that his moderate plans would promote needed change without destabilizing the economy and upsetting foreign business in Mexico. But when the provisions affecting foreigners appeared in the new constitution, the U.S. government pressed Carranza to protect American interests in Mexico.

PRESIDENT CARRANZA, SEATED, POSES WITH GENERAL ÁLVARO OBREGÓN. OBREGÓN SERVED AS CARRANZA'S MINISTER OF WAR BUT ORGANIZED A MILITARY REVOLT TO OVERTHROW CARRANZA IN 1920.

Many people who would benefit from the new constitution, such as agrarian and industrial workers, wanted immediate results. When Carranza proposed legislation to set up the mechanisms for land distribution, people complained. They wanted him to confiscate (take) the property and give it back immediately to the peasants. When Carranza felt that labor unions were moving too fast and trying to grasp power by striking, this was seen as a betrayal of the constitution. Change could not happen fast enough for many of the people. Carranza wanted a more measured response to the problems.

As Carranza approached the end of his presidential term, he tried to name a successor whom he could control. He hoped this would allow him to hold on to power even after his term had ended. Carranza felt it was critical to the stability of Mexico that his successor continue to follow his own strategy of slow and moderate change. He saw a real danger of return to the chaos of revolution if the pace of implementation was increased. But General Álvaro Obregón, the minister of war in Carranza's government and previously a strong Carranza supporter, declared himself a candidate for the presidency. Carranza insisted that his choice, Ignacio Bonillas, should be elected. An assassination attempt, carried out by supporters of Obregón on April 8, 1920, failed but forced Carranza to flee.

> *"[The Mexican people must] support the principles of democracy, for which we have fought during ten years."*
>
> —Venustiano Carranza, 1920

Obregón organized a military revolt to overthrow Carranza. Hoping to be able to restore order, Carranza refused to step down as president of Mexico. He issued a statement in May 1920 calling on the Mexican people to "support the principles of democracy, for which we have fought during ten years." But the people did not rally to his side. A second assassination attempt on May 21, 1920, succeeded. News reports announced that Carranza was killed by his own troops.

> *"The economy was blighted, finances a bedlam, demoralization widespread."*
>
> —historian Charles Cumberland, 1972

General Obregón took office as president on December 1, 1920, after new elections were held. Obregón began to implement the constitutional mandates vigorously. "Obregón took over an exhausted and disheveled country," noted historian Charles C. Cumberland. "The economy was blighted, finances a bedlam, demoralization widespread." Carranza had not been able to move the country forward. However, Obregón spent his four years in office beginning the much-needed changes in all the areas mandated by the constitution. His successor, Plutarcho Elías Calles, moved even more quickly in redistributing land. The country was finally making measurable progress in addressing long-standing societal problems. Mexico was in recovery, but the revolution had drained the country's resources and its people.

> *"[Workers should be able to] fight for the*
> *betterment of their conditions."*
>
> —Mexican president Álvaro Obregón, December 1, 1920

THE COST OF REVOLUTION

The Mexican Revolution did not come without costs. There were financial costs. There were also high human costs. In 2001 historian Robert McCaa of the University of Minnesota Population Center studied the documentation available on the demographics (or population statistics) of Mexico from 1910 to 1920, the official period of the revolution. Other historians, he said, gave "Total losses . . . from 1.9 to 3.5 million" people. After extensive study, he estimated that approximately 3 million Mexicans lost their lives over the ten-year period of the revolution. This amounted to about one-fifth of Mexico's 15 million people.

Some of the deaths resulted from the fighting. However, many were from the disruption caused by the fighting as the poor lost any means of supporting themselves. Historian Oscar J. Martínez recorded deaths by "malnutrition, disease, lack of medical care, and other hardships." He noted that "hundreds of thousands faced poverty and destitution," along with "recurring food shortages" as the fighting disrupted the economy year after year.

Historian Adolfo Gilly gives a conservative estimate of one million deaths from not only the fighting, but also "the declining birth-rate, the flight northwards [to the United States] from the effects of civil war." He described an economy affected by "violent changes [that] . . . disorganized the railway network," destroying the infrastructure that was required to keep food and other necessities flowing.

Mexicans had lived through ten years of war— "guerrilla war, peasant war, religious war, civil war," according to historians Donald Hodges and Ross Gandy. It left them exhausted but victorious. In the revolution's aftermath, the Mexican people could finally leave behind the years of fighting and hope to see the goals of their revolution become reality.

CHAPTER 4

Hope for the Peons

L AND AND LAND OWNERSHIP were at the heart of the Mexican Revolution. So were conditions affecting the peons who worked the land and those who left for the cities in search of better-paying jobs. In the aftermath of the revolution, and with a new constitution, the peons of the countryside and the cities hoped for changes that would improve their lives.

As the Laws Changed

Land reform would have to be comprehensive to meet the goals of the revolution. It would have to cause a revolutionary shift in the economic power structure of the country. This would not be an easy transition. Agrarian reform may have been the battle cry of the revolution, but there was no concrete plan to implement the changes when the revolution ended. This lack of a specific plan for change was one reason the revolution lasted so long. There were serious disagreements over the pace and extent of agrarian reform.

Emiliano Zapata and his Zapatistas had perhaps the clearest plan of any of the revolutionaries. Over the course of the revolution, beginning as early as 1911, Zapata had distributed land to peasants who had owned land before the hacendados. Around Morelos, in the south-central part of Mexico, for example, he captured land and turned it over to land commissions, which he created. It was the job of these commissions to distribute the land fairly to its previous owners. He monitored their work carefully to make sure they were properly carrying out their task. He also worked to establish a bank that would loan money to the peasants so that they could buy farming tools and materials. Later government programs, begun after the adoption of the new constitution, followed his example.

EMILIANO ZAPATA, SEATED CENTER, POSES WITH SOME OF HIS ZAPATISTAS IN 1914. THROUGHOUT THE REVOLUTION, ZAPATA RETURNED LAND TO PEASANTS WHO HAD LOST LAND TO THE HACENDADOS.

The Constitution of 1917 did not give the Zapatistas all that they wanted, but it did provide "for the restitution [return] of land which had been illegally alienated [taken from them]," and, more importantly, "for the granting of additional lands to those communities which could not attain sufficient land for their needs." If this could be implemented correctly, the constitution would solve both sides of the problem. It would restore the land wrongfully taken from the Mexican people. But it would also make sure that the people were given enough good-quality agricultural land to allow for self-sufficiency so that they were not forced back into peonage.

MAKING IT WORK

The new laws also created a National Agrarian Commission with nine appointed members. Its job was to administer the transition. It oversaw local commissions with five members each. They were tasked with studying specific areas and recommending what should be done to right the wrongs of the past. The land to be distributed would be turned over to village groups as communal property rather than to individuals. The villagers themselves would have control of the property and make decisions on its use as a community.

> "[A Mexican village could submit a petition asking] that justice be done by a return of its old lands."
>
> —historian Frank Tannenbaum, 1929

To begin the process, a village would submit a request for the return of its land. Its petition would ask "that justice be done by a return of its old lands," according to a study of the system published by the Brookings Institution in 1929. The village officials would include any documents that might prove former ownership of the land. Villages could also petition to receive additional land to make themselves sustainable. Once the land was surveyed and titled, the process could begin within each village for either dividing the land among the inhabitants of the village or creating a communal arrangement known as an *ejido*.

FAST FACT

ABOUT ONE-QUARTER OF THE LAND UNDER CULTIVATION IN MEXICO IS STILL COMMUNALLY OWNED.

The ejido is an old concept in Mexico, one that dates back to the Aztecs before the Spanish arrived. Under an ejido, the people of a community work the land together and share the profits of their labor. Many ejidos were created during this period of land redistribution.

The process of distribution was uneven at first. Setting up the commissions was difficult, as there were not many people with the skills needed to serve on the commissions. Many villages lacked the know-how to be able to develop their petition for the local commission. Implementation was slowed by the lack of education among those who were filing land claims. However, the system began functioning more effectively during the presidency of Plutarcho Elías Calles, whose term began in 1924. Calles loosened some of the bureaucratic rules and procedures. He also made it clear to the commissions that he expected results. He recognized that his political survival rested on his ability to successfully distribute the

MEXICAN FARMERS, MEMBERS OF AN EJIDO, ARE SHOWN BRINGING THEIR CORN TO MARKET IN THIS 1905 PHOTO.

land. "To keep the agrarians happy," noted historian William Weber Johnson, "Calles began expropriating [taking] and distributing land at a record breaking rate. By the end of his administration he would have distributed 3,088,000 hectares [7,630,448 acres]."

Agrarian reform could not be accomplished quickly or painlessly. It was not possible to transform within a period of years an entire economic system that had been in place for centuries. It was also not possible for an illiterate peasantry to become self-sufficient landowners with just a few years of education. The process of change was difficult, especially in the early years.

WORKERS IN THE CITIES

Agrarian reform liberated the peasantry. Peons were given a role in determining their own destiny through the redistribution of the land wealth in the country. That role also helped ensure that they had some voice in the political process for the first time.

The rural peasants were not the only ones who benefited from change in the aftermath of the revolution. The workers in the cities also experienced improvements in living conditions, thanks to protections and rights provided in the new constitution.

Workers toiling in the mining and petroleum industries had grievances (complaints) with the old system. These grievances were similar to those of peasants who worked on farms. They could not support themselves on the wages they earned. As with the rural peasants, this resulted in a form of involuntary servitude. Unlike the peasants in the countryside, however, their small numbers did not give them a strong voice in the early stages of the revolution. As the revolution matured, they aligned themselves with Carranza, seeing him as their best hope for change.

The workers had created an organization, the Casa del Obrero Mundial (COM), which spoke on their behalf. Founded in 1912, the labor organization brought together small groups of laborers so that they could make their grievances known to the government. It allied itself with Carranza in the fight to overthrow Huerta in 1914. As it grew stronger, the COM called for the government to take over all industry and give control to the workers. The leaders of the COM were Marxists, members of a worldwide movement that advocated the overthrow of oppressive governments and the institution of rule by the workers. The favored method of achieving this goal was to call for a widespread strike that would shut down all of a country's industries, creating economic chaos. In the turmoil, the workers could seize the governmental offices and take over the country.

Feeling that their voices were being ignored, in 1916 workers in Mexico City declared a general strike. Having supported Carranza in the past, they expected favorable treatment by him. This did not happen. Instead, their strike was suppressed and martial law

FEDERAL TROOPS PATROL THE STREETS OF MEXICO CITY. PRESIDENT CARRANZA DECLARED MARTIAL LAW AFTER A GENERAL STRIKE BY WORKERS IN 1916.

(rule by the army) was imposed in Mexico City. Historian John Lear wrote of the "blame and despair" that "reverberated [was felt] among working-class leaders" as they faced the consequences of their decision to strike. But the workers, he noted, had not given up. Their newspaper, *Luz,* urged them on: "Don't believe that our ardor for the struggle has fallen."

Despite the unsuccessful strike, the workers' efforts paid off in the constitution that was drafted the following year. Lear noted the strong emphasis in the new constitution on workers' rights. Article 123 of the constitution "guaranteed the right to organize unions and strikes . . . established minimal work conditions and went far to restrict employer abuses of workers." It was a progressive [forward thinking] provision, going far beyond how workers were treated in other nations. The Mexican constitution set goals that called for specific worker rights, such as the right to organize into unions or the right to strike. It also incorporated protections for children in the workplace, limiting the number of hours they could work. Women were granted the right to lighter duties in the latter months of pregnancy and rest periods for nursing their babies when they returned to work after giving birth. All workers were to have an eight-hour work day that guaranteed a livable wage. Workers were also entitled to receive overtime pay if they exceeded the standard workday.

The new constitution contained bold provisions for workers, but many of these were not carried out. Three years after its adoption, when General Obregón took office, labor was finding that actually making changes would not be easy. Wages were still low and patience with the government was waning. On assuming office, President Obregón publicly recognized the right of the workers to "fight for the betterment of their conditions." He promised to introduce laws that would raise wages. He also promised laws that would give work-

PRESIDENT ÁLVARO OBREGÓN POSES AT HIS WRITING DESK IN THIS
1921 PORTRAIT. UPON TAKING OFFICE, OBREGÓN PROMISED TO RAISE
WAGES AND GIVE WORKERS RETIREMENT BENEFITS.

ers retirement benefits and financial protection if they suffered inju-
ries on the job. He promised to make the needs of labor a priority
for his presidency.

In spite of his support, the legislation was years in coming. The
first comprehensive labor bill was not passed until 1931. It was called

the Federal Labor Act, and it marked the first law ever in Mexico "to define general labor, as well as safety and health standards, for the Mexican workplace." The law would be strengthened as the years passed. Labor unions, such as the Confederation of Mexican Workers (Confederación de Trabajadores de México, the CTM), were founded in 1936 to push for improved working conditions. The CTM worked closely with the leading political party in Mexico to see that progress continued.

The peasants in the countryside and the workers in the cities had won recognition of their rights with the adoption of the 1917 constitution. However, measurable economic gains did not come quickly or easily. Both groups, however, could point to slow, steady improvements in their ability to earn a living in the aftermath of the Revolution.

CHAPTER 5

Diminished Church, Educated Peasantry

THE AFTERMATH OF THE REVOLUTION brought chang-
es to other aspects of life in Mexico. Before the adoption of
the constitution, Catholicism played a part in every facet of daily
life—from government decision making to education to religion to
cultural expression. Under the new constitution, Mexico adopted a
secular, nonreligious govern-
ment, separating the functions
of church and state. This was a
huge change for Mexico, and it
led to unrest. This one change
brought to the common people
of Mexico an opportunity that
had not existed before. The poor
were offered new and improved
schools that would impact their

FAST FACT

ABOUT 75 MILLION
PEOPLE, OR 88 PERCENT
OF MEXICO'S POPULATION,
IS CATHOLIC. THIS
REPRESENTS THE SECOND
LARGEST POPULATION OF
CATHOLICS IN THE WORLD,
SURPASSED ONLY BY
BRAZIL.

levels of literacy and education. With education they could increase their ability to function politically as full members of their society. They would also have the knowledge and tools to determine their own economic destinies.

THE NEW WORLD OF THE CONSTITUTION

Many of those who supported the revolution called for the separation of church and state. They believed that separating the functions of church and state could offer a better way to meet the needs of the citizens, one that would be fair to all beliefs and would support the needs of the poor. This point of view won full support at the constitutional convention. This was a tremendous loss for the Catholic Church, which lost both power and influence in government.

The Catholic Church lost more than political power and influence. It lost control over decision making in religious matters. Perhaps more important, it also lost its right to exist and minister to the people of Mexico. "Monastic vows [to become a monk or a nun] and religious Orders were prohibited, and the Church and the clergy [priesthood] were deprived of the right to own property, teach, or vote" wrote historian Jean A. Meyer.

The constitution had set up conflict between the church and the new government. The new constitution had taken away the rights of the church to minister to a population that was overwhelmingly Catholic. How would this population cope when they suddenly lost their priests, their churches, and their right to worship? The answer depended on how Mexico's presidents handled the changes. A slow pace could mean time for both sides to adjust to the new circumstances. Compromises could be worked out that

The Church in Politics

IN MOST PARTS OF THE MODERN developed world, the role of churches is primarily religious. This is not the only role that the church has played historically. In the past, it was common for people to recognize little separation between church and state. In fact, religious leaders often possessed at least as much political influence as government officials.

In part, this was because the clergy was also the best-educated segment of society. Therefore, it was common for religious leaders to serve as chancellors (advisers) to the various kings of European nations. The pope, the head of the Catholic Church, was a head of state also. His kingdom of the Papal States fielded an army and was recognized among the nation-states of Europe during the Middle Ages and Renaissance.

Mexico, settled by the strongly Catholic nation of Spain, followed the Catholic European model for governing. Even the English, who were the most Protestant of kingdoms, automatically set up an official state religion in their colonies. The establishment of the separation of church and state as the first amendment to the United States Constitution and in Mexico in the early 1900s represented a dramatic break from historical practice. Such separation was a truly revolutionary concept.

would allow the church to continue in its ministerial role. Church and state could negotiate the transfer of the educational function to the secular government. This would allow the process of creating a new school infrastructure to take place without disrupting the entire education system.

Strict and immediate implementation, on the other hand, could mean violent confrontation. This is what happened when Plutarcho Elías Calles became president on December 1, 1924. In 1926, President Calles began enforcing the new constitutional provisions. He submitted new laws to congress regarding the rights of the clergy. The law that passed in June 1926, the Law for Reforming the Penal

Code, was extreme. Among other provisions, it fined anyone wearing clerical garb in public. It set penalties for any priest who in any way criticized the government. It also expelled from the country all foreign-born clergy. All church property was nationalized, or put under control of the government.

THE CRISTERO REBELLION

These actions triggered warfare in a conflict known as the Cristero Rebellion, or the Cristiada. At first, the Catholic Church organized peaceful resistance to the new legislation. Church leaders called for a general strike to begin on August 1, 1926. All church worship in the country was suspended. The church encouraged Catholics to refuse to participate in society. Catholic teachers were encouraged to refuse to teach in public schools. Catholics were asked to boycott (avoid) the use of public transportation and to stop attending civil activities such as plays and movies. The quiet boycott lasted a few months but had little effect. Catholic bishops also worked through the political system, pushing for amendments that would allow them more freedoms. However, President Calles's law had made it a punishable offense to question the current system. Violent confrontation resulted. "Since they [church and state] both strove for universal domination [absolute control]," wrote Meyer, "the war was bound to be total."

Government troops attacked a parish (neighborhood) church holding illegal services on August 4, 1926. In the attack, the parish priest was killed. Catholics were shocked, and the level of violence grew. Active warfare itself came on January 1, 1927, when a group of rebels began attacking the countryside. They called themselves the Cristeros, or Christ fighters. With their cries of "Viva Cristo Rey!"[Long Live Christ the King] and "Viva la Virgen de Guadalupe!" [Long Live the Virgin of Guadalupe], the Cristeros began to take over large swaths of rural land in Mexico. They occupied small villages, interfered with train service, and stole supplies from ranches. Against the local militia (citizen army) troops, called Agraristas, they were often successful. The Cristeros even included female fighters. Some historians estimate that as many as ten thousand women joined the fight against the government. At times the active fighters numbered more than fifty thousand men in the field.

Hoping to avoid direct confrontation with the government, church leaders never voiced official support for the Cristeros. They did, however, let everyone know that they felt the Cristero cause was a moral one. With emotions running high on both sides, some of the fighting became quite brutal as government troops were sent in to deal with the problem. Many civilians and clergy found

Our Lady of Guadalupe

THE PATRON SAINT OF MEXICO is Our Lady of Guadalupe. In 1531 Juan Diego, fifty-seven years old and a poor, indigenous worker, was walking on Tepeyac Hill in Mexico City when he saw a vision of a woman who told him to build a church right at that spot and to dedicate it to the Blessed Mother (the Virgin Mary, mother of Jesus). Juan could not convince the local bishop that he had indeed seen the Blessed Mother. The bishop felt that she would never come to a poor local man with a request. She would instead have appeared to the bishop himself.

When the vision reappeared to Juan Diego on December 12, the bishop was forced to accept Juan Diego's account. A shrine to the Blessed Mother as Our Lady of Guadalupe was built on the spot where she appeared. Her feast day of December 12 has been observed in Mexico ever since,as well as in parts of the United States where Mexican cultural influence is strong, such as California, New Mexico, and Texas.

A GROUP OF WOMEN CRISTEROS POSE WITH THEIR WEAPONS IN THIS PHOTO FROM THE 1920S. THOUSANDS OF MEXICAN WOMEN JOINED THE CRISTEROS IN SUPPORT OF THE CATHOLIC CHURCH.

themselves caught between the rebels and government troops. A Carmelite sister (a nun of the Carmelite order), Mother Elías de Santa Sacto, escaped from Mexico during the rebellion and then shared her story of what she referred to as outrages. "All the communities of nuns have been expelled from the entire Republic, being given but a half-hour to leave and not allowed to take with them a change of clothes, and in many cases not even a breviary [prayer book]." She also detailed instances of physical abuse of the nuns by soldiers, including those made "victims of the unbridled [uncontrolled] passions of the soldiers."

The conflict continued over the next two years. Finally, an American diplomat, Dwight Morrow, convinced President Calles to accept a negotiated settlement. This settlement restored property and some control of issues of worship to the Catholic Church. More than ninety thousand people had perished over the course of this rebellion. Many of those were priests who refused to stop their work.

MEXICAN PRESIDENT PLUTARCO CALLES, RIGHT, GREETS AMERICAN DIPLOMAT DWIGHT MORROW IN 1927. MORROW CONVINCED CALLES TO ACCEPT A NEGOTIATED SETTLEMENT WITH THE CRISTEROS.

A number of them were later canonized (named as saints) by the Catholic Church for accepting death rather than deserting their duties to their parishioners (those who worship at a parish church).

THE CHURCH AND STATE COMPROMISE

The Cristero rebellion officially came to an end in 1929. The response among the people of Mexico was immediate. The *New York Times* on June 24, 1929, reported "vast spontaneous demonstrations going on throughout Mexico today in gratitude for the peace between State and Church." The crisis was over, and religious services resumed in the country.

Outbreaks of rebellion continued in some areas for a number of years. Catholic priests were harassed and sometimes persecuted as they went about their work. Conditions were bad enough that many priests left the country. Historians estimate that the number of active priests went from forty-five hundred at the beginning of the Calles church reform period to around three hundred by 1934. It took a new president to bring real peace to Mexico on the issue of church-state relations. President Lázaro Cárdenas, who took office in 1934, explicitly promised not to enforce the provisions of the constitution concerning the Catholic Church. In a speech in 1936, he said that "It is no concern of the government to undertake antireligious campaigns."

A MEXICAN IDENTITY

While the Catholic Church finally regained its footing in the spiritual life of Mexico, it did not regain control over the country's educational system. José Vasconcelos, a lawyer who had been an early supporter of Madero and who had worked to secularize education, was given the task of creating a nonreligious educational system and forging a new cultural identity for Mexico.

Vasconcelos had long advocated the need for Mexicans to see themselves as one people. He wanted to develop a cultural identity that merged Mexico's rich pre-Columbian heritage with the cultural contributions of their Spanish conquerors and the unique tribal identities of a large, diverse group of indigenous peoples. Most Mexicans

PRESIDENT LÁZARO CÁRDENAS ASKED JOSÉ VASCONCELOS, BELOW, TO DEVELOP A NEW EDUCATIONAL SYSTEM AND CULTURAL IDENTITY FOR MEXICO.

had no sense of being part of Mexico. They did not have a common language in which to discuss their differences. There were about ninety indigenous languages in use around the country, and many speakers spoke only their native language. Vasconcelos had often called on the government to adopt a common language for schools throughout the country. This, he believed, would help foster unity and a sense of national identity. At the same time, he knew that this coming together of cultures had to respect those individual aspects of each of the varied indigenous tribal groups and preserve their uniqueness. The constitution had mandated a pluriculture, a culture that melded together the various groups while allowing them to keep their uniqueness.

This was a monumental task, one that could only be achieved in Mexico in the aftermath of the revolution. It reflected an ideal that had probably never been achieved on the scale that was intended here. To begin this task, the government focused on the one concrete element—education—that could set the stage for developing a sense of Mexican-ness. The first step had to be education to create a literate population with a common language. Then Mexicans could learn about the rest of their country and its history and culture.

To Educate a Nation

Historian Adrian A. Bantjes calls the Mexican Revolution "a cultural revolution . . . which sought to reshape local culture, identity, and everyday life." The constitution of 1917 was specific in its requirements for education. Education would be universal for all children in the country, meaning all children would be provided with access to education. Requirements for attendance and availability of education after the primary level would vary from region to region, especially as the new system was being organized. The government would also try to educate adults through literacy programs geared to their needs. And because the Catholic Church would no longer play a part in education, the state or provincial governments would fund the schools and provide the means for education to take place. It also meant, however, that the aim was to make "State functions . . . take precedence over those of the Church" and to create "two spheres in society, the temporal [the worldly state] and the spiritual." The Church would remain the primary religious force in the lives of the people. But it would not be the entity that educated the people, and its holy days would not necessarily be recognized as the country's national holidays.

> # FAST FACT
>
> MODERN MEXICO HAS A 90 PERCENT LITERACY RATE, RANKING IT IN THE TOP HALF OF ALL COUNTRIES AND ABOVE THE WORLD AVERAGE RATE OF 82 PERCENT.

This new program required the right person to lead the way. José Vasconcelos was named minister of education in 1921. Vasconcelos was a man with a vision of what education could do for Mexico. He had already made a name for himself by advocating for developing a Spanish language culture in Mexico and in all of Latin America. He saw the potential for creating a regional bloc that could be strong enough to counter the influence of the United States.

Vasconcelos viewed his most critical challenge as bringing the indigenous peoples into the educational system. This would give them skills to improve economically. However, Vasconcelos saw another aspect of educating the indigenous peoples as even more critical. He wished to fully integrate the indigenous peoples into a unified Mexican society. As he told a visiting American newsman in 1921,

"They must be brought in touch with the rest of us. . . . Unless we become as one people, how can our aspirations harmonize?"

With a vision for change already in mind, Vasconcelos was the perfect choice to begin the modernization and secularization of the Mexican educational system in the aftermath of the revolution. In just a few years, he arranged construction of more than one thousand schools in rural areas. However, he went further than just concerning himself with the education of the young. He also focused on bringing the existing post-school age population to literacy. Historian Call noted that he "organized and sent cultural missions . . . into the primitive backlands to show villagers the way to a better life." These missions taught the peasants basic reading and writing skills. The missions also helped them develop other skills needed in the workplace.

Vasconcelos had studied the criticisms of foreign companies that had described native workers as lazy and unproductive. What he saw was not laziness but a basic lack of understanding of the needs of the workplace on the part of the peasants. According to his biographer, Luis A. Marentes, Vasconcelos felt that, with training, the poor living in rural areas could "acquire the technical skills necessary for their incorporation into the modern capitalist economy." Employers had complained that Mexican workers were unreliable or lazy when they refused to follow work rules. Vasconcelos saw that the problem was that many workers did not understand the need to work on a fixed time clock schedule. He created programs that taught workers to arrive at work when scheduled and to work the full day. Workers were also taught that they would have to forego their traditional afternoon siesta (rest period).

NEW RESOURCES FOR EDUCATION

Vasconcelos also knew that the task of educating the populace would require vast new resources in terms of buildings, supplies,

MEXICAN PEASANTS, YOUNG AND OLD, LEARN TO SPEAK, READ, AND WRITE IN SPANISH. JOSÉ VASCONCELOS BELIEVED THAT ADVANCEMENTS WOULD COME ONCE MEXICO'S PEOPLE SHARED A COMMON LANGUAGE.

and teachers. Education had previously accounted for less than 1 percent of the national budget. He successfully lobbied to raise that total to 15 percent. He also insisted that all students be taught Spanish rather than be allowed to learn in their own native language. This was a controversial change since no one had ever attempted to teach all Mexican children in a common language.

With so many languages in use around the country, even basic communication was a problem. Vasconcelos theorized that a common language would encourage people to feel part of their country and see themselves as a united nation. His purpose in adopting this approach, his biographer noted, was so that the schools would "incorporate their pupils into the broader national community and . . . foster patriotism."

Vasconcelos's vision placed education within a broader cultural context. In addition to his literacy programs for adults and to classes in basic skills, he created libraries throughout the country. He encouraged artists and musicians to celebrate Mexican culture. As a result, there was "a surge of creativity in the arts unparalleled since the pre-Columbian era . . . [that] provoked a mania for the 'truly Mexican,' and inspired countless ballads and stories which have become the modern Mexican folklore." When President Calles took office, a new education minister was named and the pace of progress slowed. However, the mechanism of change was already in motion, and that motion was unstoppable.

"Unless we become as one people, how can our aspirations harmonize?"

—minister of education José Vasconcelos, 1921

The attempt to secularize Mexico, while at the same time giving the people a sense of cultural and national identity, was moving quickly. It would take time to see whether these efforts in education and cultural awareness would be successful. Would education give the common and indigenous peoples of Mexico a sense of their citizenship? Would that translate into political power within the new Mexican state? As these new policies were implemented, no one could guess whether they would be successful. Mexico and its people were engaged in an experiment in social change that had the potential to achieve the ideals of the new constitution.

CHAPTER 6

A Government for the Mexican People

"EVEN I," WROTE EDITH O'SHAUGHNESSY to her mother on May 20, 1911, "stranger and alien, have a sort of feeling that if this revolution proves successful the 'liberties' of the Mexican people will, as usual, get lost in the mêlée [chaos]." The wife of the American ambassador to Mexico captured in one sentence all the fears and hopes for the common people of Mexico. Mexico had a long history of putting the needs of the majority of its citizens last. This was true in many aspects of official policy. It was most obvious, however,

> *"The 'liberties' of the Mexican people will, as usual, get lost in the mêlée [chaos]."*
>
> —Edith O'Shaunessy, 1911

in how little the Mexican people were able to influence events in their own country. There were two parts to this problem. One was the power that private armies held in choosing who would govern Mexico and how. The second was the long-standing practice of presidents allowing foreigners to dictate governmental decisions in return for support of the officeholder. In the aftermath of the revolution, Mexicans searched for a way to address these issues.

GOVERNMENT BY COUP D'ÉTAT

Military men had controlled events in Mexico for many years. They had fought each other for wealth and power. However, the idea of an army that fought on behalf of the nation as a whole did not exist in Mexico before or during the revolution. In Mexico, historian Edwin Lieuwen wrote, "Politics was a game played with swords and guns and the victors, more often than not, claimed the treasury as their spoil. The word 'army' became synonymous . . . with crime, venality [corruption], violence."

> *"Politics was a game played with swords and guns and the victors, more often than not, claimed the treasury as their spoil."*
>
> —Mexican historian Edwin Lieuwen, 1968

The Mexican Revolution was an example of this destructive process in action. Military coups had disrupted and destabilized Mexico from the earliest days of independence from Spain. But political stability finally came to Mexico in the revolution's aftermath. In the poetical words of one account, "Mexico tamed the beast that devours governments in Latin America—the Army." Beginning with President Obregón in 1920, systematic efforts were made to turn the army into a tool of civilian government. Obregón and others wanted to create a national military force that served the needs of the government rather than the needs of individual generals or other leaders. The revolution and the years prior to the revolution had been characterized by personal armies. There was a personal army of Villistas following Pancho Villa. There was the Liberation Army of the South made up of Zapatistas. The warring armies provided support to elect presidents and then deposed them if they did not meet their demands. There was simply too much of what one writer called "ambitious generals" trying to take the "guilded-chair [sic] in the National Palace" and become president. After a century in which political leadership often came after a military takeover, post-revolutionary Mexico finally moved away from that model of government.

President Obregón knew that this was a difficult problem that could not be solved overnight. He worked the problem from two angles. First, he brought into the government army all those who were active in private regional armies. The lure to get them to join was monetary. These new officers did not like his authority over them, but they did like the fact that he paid them extremely well.

This cost the government a fortune, some say as much as two-thirds of the country's budget.

At the same time, the president began a program of selecting promising young military leaders. He sent them to Mexico's new Military Academy in Mexico City or for military training in other countries. He was gradually building an army of professionals with loyalty to the government and not to a general who offered them a share of the spoils if they would help bring him to power. It was a method never before tried by the government, and it required patience. Obregón knew the importance of success in implementing this reform. He knew that if it succeeded, it would lead to a stable Mexican government.

MEXICAN ARMY OFFICERS ATTEND A BANQUET HELD IN THEIR HONOR. PRESIDENT OBREGÓN TRIED TO TRANSFORM THE ARMY INTO A TOOL OF CIVILIAN GOVERNMENT BY OFFERING BETTER PAY AND RECOGNITION FOR SERVICE.

To Be a Citizen

MEXICO'S HISTORY OF RULE by a strong oligarchy (rule by the few) controlling both the money and the political power was extreme, but not so unusual historically. The right to full citizenship and a voice in governing the country is still a relatively new concept.

Even in ancient Greece, which is considered to be the birthplace of democracy, full citizenship was limited. Citizens were free males who had been born in Greece and were wealthy enough to own land. Ancient Rome, which incorporated many of the Greek political concepts, allowed voting citizenship only to males who owned land. A person could have been born a slave, later be freed, eventually own property, and earn full voting rights, but only if that person was male. Women never obtained voting rights in the Roman Republic.

During the European Middle Ages and well into the Renaissance, whether a person had a voice in society was determined by economic status. Even with the advent of the Industrial Revolution and the growth of the middle class in the 1800s, women were denied voting rights in most European democratic societies until the early 1900s. Viewed in that context, the oligarchy in Mexico was very much a mirror of other societies. However, by the early twentieth century, the times were changing, and Mexico was just one of the countries where major changes in government were coming.

It would be a while before the new army was tested. But when it was, the control and reforms instituted by Obregón paid off. For example, when General Saturnine Cedillo attempted a military coup in 1938 against President Lázaro Cárdenas, he expected the regular army to support his efforts. Instead they remained loyal to the president. Historians Hodges and Gandy noted that "the Army was a new creature, staffed by officers loyal to the President, whoever he might be." The power to overthrow the government of Mexico militarily had been destroyed. In the twenty-first century, Mexico's army is proportionally one of the smallest of any Latin American country. It consumes very little of the country's economic resources. Nor does the Mexican military have a real role in the political process. No matter the political disagreements, no matter the economic issues, no matter the religious squabbles, the military has not staged a coup d'état since the official end of the revolution in 1920. The citizens of Mexico have a government determined by the ballot and not by the intervention of the military.

FOREIGNERS AT THE GATES

The other obstacle to allowing Mexicans to control their own destiny took much longer to remove. This was the role of foreign interests in Mexican society. Foreigners, particularly Americans, Britons, and Germans, had long provided economic support to the Mexican government. In return, they reaped the profits from the industries that they controlled. But they also occupied an influential position in Mexican society. In the aftermath of the revolution, little by little, they lost this position.

The 1917 constitution gave the government of Mexico the right to take control of property owned by foreign companies. The government became free to simply declare that they owned the buildings and resources and to send the foreigners managing them home. At first, the Mexican government did not act on this new right. Government officials knew that they lacked the knowledge and resources to take over the industries that had been under foreign control. But they needed to be clear that the taking of property was their right under the new constitution. So President Obregón worked, in the words of historian Charles Cumberland, "to assuage [calm] the ire [anger]of foreign investors . . . while at the same time defending . . . essential precepts [principles] of revolutionary nationalism [declaring that the country was entitled to the properties whenever it saw fit to take them]." An uneasy truce existed for a period of years.

American businessmen such as Irving Herr complained that "workmen [got] all the consideration" under the new constitution, making their jobs more difficult. Workers had won new rights in the workplace in the aftermath of the revolution. These new rights sometimes interfered with the old ways of doing things. But foreign investors were still getting a good return on their investment, so their engineers and managers were instructed to accommodate the new rules.

The mining industries were not producing as well as they had before the revolution, but "oil continued to increase in importance and to become the mainstay of the Mexican government through the taxes paid by the oil companies." Those taxes were enough of a return to justify leaving the foreigners in control of the industry for the time being. That changed when President Lázaro Cárdenas took over as president in 1934. He inherited a Mexico that was finally stable and ready to stand on its own. Foreign control of the mining and oil industries was no longer needed. Foreign interests lost their land, and the railway lines reverted to Mexican national control. Then on March 18, 1938, Cárdenas ordered the expropriation (the legal term for the taking over of a business by a government) of all of the assets of the foreign oil companies. This action followed a long labor dispute. The dispute pitted foreign-owned oil companies against the new Mexican labor unions. The unions were demanding increased wages for Mexican workers. The government sided with the labor unions after a court ruled that their demands were reasonable. The owners then threatened to

THE AFTERMATH OF THE MEXICAN REVOLUTION

PRESIDENT CÁRDENAS, AT THE MICROPHONE, ADDRESSES 250,000 PEOPLE
IN MEXICO CITY IN 1938, ANNOUNCING THAT HIS GOVERNMENT HAS
TAKEN CONTROL OF PROPERTY BELONGING TO FOREIGN OIL COMPANIES.

take their business and go home. As the dispute became increasingly hostile, Cárdenas decided that Mexico had had enough of
the foreign interests. He took control of the oil industry, and the
foreigners were sent home.

The U.S. government protested but said it would accept the decision as long as the companies received adequate compensation. The
Mexican government offered to pay compensation for the buildings

and equipment but not for the value of the oil still in the ground. This offer angered the American owners, and the dispute took several years to resolve. The final resolution favored Mexico, not the American companies. The formal negotiated settlement between the two countries did not come about until April 1942. At that time, "Mexico agreed to pay $40 million for general and agrarian claims and approximately $29 million for oil claims." The oil companies did not agree with the offer, which they felt covered only a small portion of what they were owed. U.S. president Franklin Roosevelt overruled them. The era of American investor involvement in the Mexican government finally came to an end.

MEXICO FOR THE MEXICANS

With the departure of the foreign businesses, the Mexican people were free to determine their own destinies. Foreigners lost their

The Government of Mexico

MEXICO IS COMPOSED OF thirty-one states and one federal district. People are eligible to vote at age eighteen. Mexico is ruled by a president who serves one six-year term of office. As in the United States, the president is both chief of state and head of the government.

The Mexican legislature, called the *Congreso de la Union*, has two houses—the *Camara de Senadores* (Senate), with 128 members who serve for six years, and the *Camara Federal de Diputados* (Chamber of Deputies), with 500 members who serve for three years.

The Mexican judicial system is headed by the *Suprema Corte de Justicia Nacional*, the equivalent of the United States Supreme Court. Much of Mexican law is modeled on U.S. law.

influence in the politics and economy of Mexico. Mexicans enjoyed a period in which the danger of military coups had also been eliminated. For the first time in their history, the Mexican people were the ones making the decisions. It would be Mexicans voting in free elections who would be making the decisions of who would govern them and who would represent their interests.

CHAPTER 7

Years of Change in the Aftermath of Revolution

I N THE DECADES SINCE the end of the Mexican Revolution, there have been many changes in Mexico. Changes have taken place in the areas of economics, politics, religion, and social structure. Much has also remained the same. Many of the issues that led to the revolution still exist in the twenty-first century. In fact, the only issue that is no longer a problem for Mexico is the need for stability. Transfers of political power have proceeded peacefully—or at least without military interference—since 1920. Success in other areas has fallen short of revolutionary goals or created new issues to deal with.

ECONOMIC LIFE FOR THE COMMON PEOPLE OF MEXICO

In the areas of agrarian reform and workers' rights, many feel that the goals of the revolution have not yet been realized. Zapata's biographer

Robert P. Millon is one of those who believes that the reform process is unfinished. "The peasants still clamor for land," he writes and "extremely low levels of living continue to prevail among the . . . population which lives in the countryside." The standard of living has not risen to where many hoped it would be with agrarian reform. Despite redistribution of land, a significant portion of the population still lives in poverty. And as before, a small portion of the population still controls a large portion of the nation's wealth. This group also continues to have greater political influence and access than do the poor.

Though agrarian reform has fallen short in some ways, it has succeeded in others. The aspect of agrarian reform that has been most successful is in the development of the community/village-run collective farms, the ejido. The ejidos have allowed for growing prosperity for those involved with them. Historian Tomme Clark Call focuses on the study of the considerable progress that has been made by the ejido. He notes that for those involved in the ejido, "Though thousands of landless rural Mexicans remain, as do huge individual landholdings, the peon has largely come into his own."

Agrarian reform has generally improved the lot of Mexico's peasants. Working collectively, at least some of this population has used the power of their numbers to attain more economic self-sufficiency. The original goal of revolutionary agrarian reform was about returning the land to the people from whom it had been taken unfairly.

GARBAGE SURROUNDS A POOR FARMER'S SHACK AND YARD IN THE MEXICAN COUNTRYSIDE. ABOUT 40 PERCENT OF MODERN MEXICO'S POPULATION LIVES IN POVERTY.

However, agrarian reform was about more than that. It was also about reform that would destroy the peonage system so that those subject to it could create a better life for themselves. Although life for the peons has improved, about 40 percent of Mexico's population still live in poverty. For these people, the promise of a better life remains unfulfilled. This explains the large number of Mexicans who head north to the United States, legally or illegally, in search of a better life.

Life for the average Mexican worker has improved. However, most of the improvement, important as it is, fell short of the ideals of the revolution. The winners on paper did not achieve the power

THE AFTERMATH OF THE MEXICAN REVOLUTION

in society that the constitution gave them in theory. Full citizenship in terms of voting rights became theirs. However, full citizenship did not translate into strong political influence. More than one-quarter of the people of modern Mexico are laborers. This is a significant increase since the revolution ended. Laborers are better paid and protected than at the time of the revolution, but many still live in poverty.

In the twenty-first century, Mexico is governed as a democracy. However, most of the poor in Mexico would say that living in a democratic society has not given them the power to improve their economic status. Their lot has certainly improved since the revolution. But the economic and political ideals that governed the revolution have never been fully realized for Mexico's poorest citizens.

THE CHURCH IN MEXICAN SOCIETY

The Mexican presidents following Cárdenas have continued the policy of not enforcing the anticlerical provisions of the 1917 constitution. However, those provisions have never been amended. In 1940 Mexican president Avila Camacho tried to remove all of the constitution's anticlerical language. His attempt was unsuccessful. He was able to modify some of the provisions, allowing Catholic schools to open as long as they were promoted as private schools, for example. The 1990s saw broader interpretations of the existing laws. Priests and nuns, for example, were allowed to once again wear clerical garb in public. In spite of these changes, any president of Mexico, at any time, could choose to enforce the limits on the Catholic Church that were established at the end of the revolution.

The Cowboy Pilgrimage

A RECENT STORY about the annual pilgrimage of cowboys to the Cristo Rey Monument in the Mexican state of Guanajuato illustrates the role Catholicism plays in Mexican culture. More than fifty years ago, a cowboy who had been ill for some time rode his horse to the top of the 8,500-foot mountain (2,591m) of Cubilete. At the top is a statue of Cristo Rey, or Christ the King. The ill cowboy was accompanied by a few other cowboys who went along to pray for his good health. The following year, he returned with more cowboys. The pilgrimage has since become a cultural event with thousands of cowboys riding to the top of the mountain each January. They sleep on the ground, file past the remaining pieces of the original statue from the site (which was destroyed during the Cristero Rebellion), and leave petitions in front of it. One man attending the ceremony recently came from his home in the United States, bringing with him his American-born son, who had never seen the ceremony. He told a reporter, "I came back from Texas to ride in this *cabalgata* [ceremonial procession]. A lot of these people come back from the States to show their faith here today. I brought my son . . . so that he can see for himself what our faith means to us."

The cabalgata reflects the deep religious sentiment among the Mexican people. It is a sentiment that the Mexican government and leaders of the Catholic Church have no wish to disturb.

However, Catholicism remains a vital force in the culture of the people. Well over three-quarters of the Mexican population is Catholic. Religious tensions still occasionally surface in Mexico. In the middle of the hotly contested 2006 Mexican presidential elections, Cardinal Norberto Rivera tried to be a peacemaker. The dispute over the voting results was causing great unrest in the country. People had taken to the streets in sometimes violent protests. The issue itself had been submitted to the court system for a decision. The cardinal offered to mediate between the two sides

> *"I brought my son . . . so that he can see for himself what our faith means to us."*
>
> —Marco Antonio González Guerrero, 2007

so that the issue could be resolved quickly and without further violence. Because he was seen as a supporter of Felipe Calderón (who eventually was ruled the winner), demonstrators repeatedly invaded the cathedral in Mexico City and tried to disrupt Rivera's Masses. A news account of one of the attacks quoted Mexican historian Enrique Krauze, "The mix of religion and politics is always explosive in Mexico." The Mexican revolution may be almost a century in the past. However, in some respects, Mexico has never fully resolved this issue.

> *"The mix of religion and politics is always explosive in Mexico."*
>
> —historian Enrique Krauze, 2006

EDUCATION

In the early 1960s, the Mexican government evaluated the state of the educational system to see whether it was reaching its intended constitutional goals. The study found serious problems. Almost 40 percent of the population was still illiterate and less than one-quarter of the people, especially in rural areas, had completed sixth grade. As a result of the study, the Mexican government in 1965 established seven thousand new literacy centers to educate adults who had not developed necessary reading skills as children in the Mexican school system. That initiative led to a rise in the functional literacy rate of the Mexican population to more than 90 percent by the year 2000.

However, the state of education in Mexico is still poor. The Mexican government spends about 5 percent of its budget on education. In the rural areas, where three-quarters of the stu-

STUDENTS IN MEXICO ATTEND ELEMENTARY SCHOOL THROUGH A GOVERNMENT PROGRAM THAT STRIVES TO KEEP CHILDREN IN SCHOOL BY PROVIDING FINANCIAL HELP TO THEIR FAMILIES.

dents attend school, many schools do not have enough teachers. Many teachers are not well trained. Many educators teaching in rural areas have only a secondary education themselves. As one education author noted: "Despite historical advancements and heroic efforts by educators, Mexico continues to struggle with 'rezago,' or educational failure. Millions of students are retained or drop out after primary school and secondary school. Rural communities—especially those of Indigenous people where millions of citizens speak Spanish as a second language—have high rates of poverty. In these settings, many children drop out of school to work and support their families, which contributes to a higher rate of illiteracy."

Despite the 90 percent literacy rate, one-third of adults in Mexico never complete the primary grades. And about one in seven Mexican children do not attend school at all. Fewer than one in every eight students pursues any education beyond secondary school. Education is a subject of considerable public dialogue in Mexico. As a result, increased funding is being allocated to improve facilities and instruction. New requirements enacted in the 1970s expanded the years of mandatory school attendance for all children from ages six to eighteen. Beginning in 2004, preschool was also required for all children.

MODERN MEXICAN CULTURE

Education was intended to be just one concrete step on the path to developing a true Mexican culture and identity. The education bill that encoded the vision of Minister of Education Vasconcelos in 1921 covered more than traditional areas of education. It also gave the education department control over "Museums, historical and artistic monuments, theatres and theatrical productions, moving pictures, conservatories of music and similar institutions," according to a summary provided by Vasconcelos to a reporter.

Using that mandate, Mexico has struggled to modernize without losing its traditional culture. Historian Michael C. Meyer summarized the first twenty years after the revolution as follows: "By no means did all the requisites [necessities] of the good life come to rural Mexico between 1920 and 1940, but by the latter date it was no longer accurate to suggest that rural Mexicans continued to live as they had since the days of the Spanish conquest." New schools and libraries helped the Mexican people gain an increased knowledge of their own country. Sharing a common language also

The Mexican Renaissance

IN THE AFTERMATH of the Mexican Revolution, the new emphasis on culture and diversity led to works of art that celebrated Mexican history and culture. The years from 1920 to 1950 are called the Mexican Renaissance.

The artists of this renaissance chose large fresco murals (painted on wet plaster) as the form for their art. Many of these murals were political as well as artistic statements. Some were clearly critical of the Mexican Revolution, others gloried in the events of that period. The muralists were known for their use of bold colors and realistic portraits.

Among the most famous of the muralists were Diego Rivera, José Clemente Orozco, David Alfaro Sisqueiros, and Rufino Tamayo. Many of them gained fame throughout the world. Many of the murals can be found in the United States and other countries. Orozco's twenty-four panel *The Epic of American Civilization*, for example, is located at Dartmouth College in Hanover, New Hampshire.

brought them together as a people. And, perhaps most important, there was a movement that showed respect for and wished to preserve their individual culture.

This is a process that continues. Mexico has progressed in the area of education. It has an active art and literary scene, which looks to interpreting the story of the Mexican people and their revolution through art and literature. But, it also has changed in its openness and willingness to embrace the past and incorporate it into the evolving culture of Mexico. As Nobel Prize–winning Mexican poet Octavio Paz observed, "Today . . . we have realized that countries change very slowly, and that if such changes are to be fertile they must be in harmony with the past and with the tradition of each nation. Thus Mexico must find her own road to modernity." Prerevolutionary Mexico has been called by historian Alan Knight "less a nation than a geographical expression, a mosaic of regions and communities . . . ethnically and physically fragmented, and lacking common national sentiments." Language and culture divided rather than united the diverse people living in the country.

In the aftermath of the revolution, the Mexican people have developed more of an identity and pride in a common heritage. It is a heritage that recognizes, in the words of historians Daniel Levy and Gabriel Székely, that "the Indian was . . . not an exotic savage, but . . . a mature person—even the source of all that was good in Mexico." Here, as in other areas of the revolutionary ideals, the development of a unified identity is still a work in progress. But this revolutionary ideal is closer to being reached.

FOREIGN INTERVENTION

As a revolutionary goal, the expulsion of the rich foreign economic interests from Mexico was fulfilled with the nationalization policies of

The North American Free Trade Agreement (NAFTA)

ON JANUARY 1, 1994, a new trade agreement went into effect that governs goods traded among the United States, Canada, and Mexico. The agreement has led to a great increase in the amount of trade between the United States and Mexico. The trade has been beneficial for the Mexican economy, where studies by the World Bank (an international organization that gives financial and technical aid to developing countries) show that real income has grown and poverty rates have improved in Mexico under the agreement.

Mexican industry, especially that involved in making parts for automobiles, has particularly thrived under the agreement. Mexican agriculture has also benefited, but not to such a great extent as industry. NAFTA remains controversial. Many people feel it has caused economic problems in the United States. Others see it as not having achieved as great an economic result as expected in poverty-ridden Mexico. Controversial or not, it has given a much needed boost to the Mexican economy.

President Cárdenas in the 1930s. With the American companies out of Mexico, the relationship between the two countries settled into a more stable pattern. But that does not mean that all of the results of this policy were good for Mexico. In prerevolutionary Mexico, the issue was foreign money coming into the economy and exploiting the people to generate a profit. Although that issue is resolved, the Mexican economy has not proved strong enough to provide a reasonable standard of living for its people.

That failure was bound to have an impact on the country that shares a long border with Mexico, the United States. Economic conditions in Mexico have directly fueled the rise in the number of Mexicans who leave their homeland because they cannot earn a decent wage there. No foreign country feels the impact of this failure of the revolutionary objectives more than the United States. If the ideals of the revolution had come to pass, the vast majority of Mexicans would be financially self-sufficient. It had been hoped that land redistribution and improvements in labor conditions would allow the people to move up the economic ladder.

Mexico remains, however, a very poor society. For this reason, many Mexicans seek a better life north of the border. Estimates vary as to the number of people who enter the United States illegally from Mexico each year. U.S. Census Bureau statistics estimate that some 8 to 9 million undocumented immigrants are currently living in the United States and that more than half of them are from Mexico. An estimated 1 million cross into the United States each year. This will probably continue until Mexico resolves its economic problems.

WHY ECONOMIC CHANGE DID NOT MEAN POLITICAL POWER

For each of the issues that led to the Mexican Revolution, strong remedies were put into place in the new constitution. Many changes have occurred that have been useful. But in every case, the changes have fallen short of the goals of the revolutionaries and of those who wrote the constitution in 1917. There are many reasons for this. Some of those goals are lofty ideals that are not achieved in any society. Some of them, such as economic goals, are not entirely under the control of the Mexican government, but rather are world economic issues.

However, there is one organization that, in the aftermath of the revolution, has had the most impact on why the revolutionary goals have not been met. That is the Institutional Revolutionary Party, or PRI (in Spanish the Partido Nacional Revolucionario, or PNR), which governed Mexico almost to the present and controlled the pace of change in Mexico in the aftermath of the revolutionary years.

The PRI was started by President Calles in 1929 and supported the goals of the revolution. But it did so by taking control of the political process. Mexico became a country with one political party, as it had in the days of the Porfiriato before the revolution. Having one political party is almost always a problem for a country's citizens because it does not give the people the choices needed to make changes in their government and its policies.

This was definitely the case with the PRI, which became a sort of shadow government. The party picked the candidates for president who would follow what the party leaders wanted done. This system works only when the party leadership really does represent the best needs of the people. This system often suffers from party leaders who come to represent only their own interests and the needs of their friends. Over time the PRI was accused of ignoring the needs of the people, being corrupt, and making it look like the people had choices while the party actually only favored the few who were part of the party leadership.

Although many good changes had come to Mexico in the aftermath of the revolution, this one party was preventing the people from having the political power that they needed to protect themselves and become full citizens in a democracy. But it was hard to break the one-party system. It was not until 2000 that a Mexican president, Vicente Fox, was elected who was not from the PRI.

CHANGE—GOOD AND BAD

The Mexican Revolution is a distant memory to those who live in the Mexico of the twenty-first century. But Mexico continues to face economic and political issues that prevent the dreams of the revolutionaries from being realized. As with most political upheavals, change brings both good and bad results. The aftermath of the Mexican Revolution is no different. The people of Mexico have traveled far from the turmoil of the revolutionary years. In many areas, they have farther yet to travel.

The Continuing Revolution

A LMOST ONE HUNDRED YEARS after the revolution of 1910, historians still debate its precise end. Was it February 5, 1917, when President Carranza signed and announced the new constitution? Was it when Obregón assumed power? Or was it some twenty years later, when many of the revolutionary reforms began to bear fruit? Or has it ever ended?

The constitution granted the Mexican people the things they had been fighting for—agrarian reform, workers' rights, a secular nation, and recognition of the country's diverse population. It was indeed a glorious day for Mexico! But, when we fast-forward to 1920, we find President Carranza refusing to resign the presidency. He enjoys the power he has been able to wield as president, and he does not want to give it up quite yet. He is willing to step aside and rule through his hand-selected candidate. Unfortunately for Carranza, the person who wins the election is his old friend Álvaro Obregón. This old friend has become his enemy. Carranza, in the great Mexican tradition, tries to stage a coup d'état and remain in power. So much for the end of the revolution and its violent changes of government having ended with the new constitution!

Do we then say that the revolution ended in 1920 simply because it was the last time that presidential power was transferred violently? Officially in the history books, the dates of the revolution are given as 1910 to 1920. It was in 1920 that Álvaro Obregón began making the constitutional changes mandated in 1917.

President Obregón was the first president of Mexico to put laws in place that would allow the goals of the constitution to become reality. But the changes took time. So it is not surprising that many

PRESIDENT CÁRDENAS MEETS WITH LABOR LEADERS IN 1938 TO DISCUSS PROBLEMS STEMMING FROM HIS GOVERNMENT'S DECISION TO TAKE CONTROL OF FOREIGN OIL HOLDINGS.

say that the years between 1920 and 1940 should be seen as a continuation of the revolution. They dispute those who say that the process of revolution ended either in 1917 or 1920. Others look at the revolution and divide it into two distinct periods. They say there was a militaristic portion of the revolution from 1910 to 1917. This was followed by a constitutional period that lasted until 1934. For these historians, the revolution continues until President Cárdenas assumes office and decides to implement the nationalization of industries. This action completes the constitutional mandate to oust foreigners from power in Mexico. Until this point, one of the great goals of the revolution had not been dealt with. The removal of foreign interests from Mexican economic life showed that all of the demands of the revolutionaries had been addressed.

That did not mean that everything had been perfectly implemented or that life was radically better in Mexico than in the prerevolutionary days. But it did mean that the country was committed to and working on the goals set forth at the constitutional convention in 1917.

When you have a revolution that was never a classic battle between two armies, it is indeed difficult to pick an ending point. The terrible disruptions of the 1910s came to a halt after the assassination of Carranza. This is when relative stability began to return to Mexico. In the years since, there has been great progress in all of the areas of dispute that led to the revolution in the first place. But the question of whether the revolution achieved all that it sought to and whether it ever will be able to do so remains open.

THE UNFINISHED BUSINESS OF REVOLUTION

"We are fed up with being robbed, fed up with fraud," stated a quote in a *New York Times* article, "We are ready for it to come to blows. .

THE AFTERMATH OF THE MEXICAN REVOLUTION

. . They want a revolution, then they'll have a revolution." The date of the article was September 6, 2006. The Mexican Revolution had been over for almost ninety years. But the talk was still of revolution. A contested presidential election in which the losing candidate charged that the voting had been rigged to defeat him was enough to bring about talk of revolution.

> *"We are fed up with being robbed, fed up with fraud. We are ready for it to come to blows. . . . They want a revolution, then they'll have a revolution."*
>
> —Saul Pérez, 2006

The Mexican presidential elections of 2006 illustrate the difficult situation in which Mexico still finds itself. Major changes for the better have taken place in the country in the years since the 1917 constitution became the law of the land. Most observers would agree with historian Howard F. Cline that Mexicans have experienced "rising standards of living, more and cheaper food, wider job opportunities . . . that seemed quite improbable in 1910 and still beyond their grasp as late as 1940."

However, despite the level of improvement, conditions in Mexico remain far behind what they should be. Half of the Mexican people earn only about twenty dollars a week, while one-tenth of the population still controls half of the wealth of the country. Historian Susan Kaufman Purcell pointed out that "although the economy grew

rapidly, so did the gap between the rich and the poor. By the 1980s, Mexico's distribution of resources was one of the most highly skewed in the hemisphere." Like their ancestors of a hundred years ago, the vast majority of Mexicans still struggle to support themselves and their families.

Mexico's progress in the aftermath of the revolution has been very uneven. In the 1990s, economic conditions led to strikes and other civil unrest. During these times, another revolution seemed possible. Many indigenous Mexicans, unhappy about the economy, came together in the Mexican state of Chiapas in 1994 to form

THE AFTERMATH OF THE MEXICAN REVOLUTION

the Zapatista Army of National Liberation. This was an echo of the private, revolutionary armies that had torn Mexico apart during the revolutionary years. This new army successfully took control in several towns. However, the Mexican government quickly put down the rebellion using federal troops. Although defeated, the group survives as a political movement to try to further support the needs of indigenous people in Mexico. The Zapatista Army of National Liberation and other like-minded groups accuse the government of being unwilling to give real power to the people.

Social and economic inequity still exist in Mexico in the twenty-first century, although some progress has been made in incorporating all the voices of Mexico into one government. Historian Daniel Levy disagrees with those who say "that Mexico merely switched one elite for another, that the plight of the masses was not substantially improved." He sees instead a revolution in which "a fossilized [rigid] oligarchy was replaced by a much broader ruling elite." He sees the progress that has been made, especially in the areas of literacy and political participation through voting.

In some ways, critics on both sides of this argument are correct. There was a change to a more active and larger voting population. It was a change that allowed for more middle-class participation in government. But many Mexicans have been left behind.

Mexico remains a divided country, both economically and politically. Wealth is still unbalanced, with a relatively small proportion of the population controlling a disproportionate amount. Many

FAST FACT

IN 2006, ALMOST 42 MILLION VOTES WERE CAST IN THE MEXICAN PRESIDENTIAL ELECTION. THIS REPRESENTED 39 PERCENT OF ALL REGISTERED VOTERS.

of the poor of Mexico still cannot make a living wage in their own country and must search elsewhere for a solution to their financial crisis. The presidential elections of 2006 illustrated the chasm that exists between those in power and those who feel their voices are ignored.

In each of the major areas that were the focus of the Mexican Revolution, historians can cite great change and progress. Agrarian reform has been successful. There has been a substantial growth in educational opportunities, which have resulted in impressive increases in literacy rates. The blatant interference in Mexican political and economic affairs by foreign powers has ended. The Catholic Church has lost its powerful role within the government and its influence on the educational system. Many more citizens have an effective voice in government than prior to the revolution.

Despite these gains, Mexico could easily return to a state of revolution, as the calls for change in the presidential election showed. For many Mexicans, the revolutionary gains are hard to see. For them the revolution in their economic and political circumstances has not arrived. As long as "a sizable segment of the nation's population continues to have little or no influence over the political process," in the words of observer Howard Handelman, another revolution in Mexico is possible. No revolution came after the Mexican courts named Felipe Calderón the winner of the contested 2006 presidential

MEXICAN PRESIDENT FELIPE CALDERÓN LEAVES THE NATIONAL CONGRESS UNDER HEAVY SECURITY AFTER HIS INAUGURATION ON DECEMBER 1, 2006.

election. On December 1, 2006, he took office and the immediate electoral crisis passed. However, that did not mean that the supporters of Andrés Manuel López Obrador's candidacy stopped believing that the election had been fraudulent and the vote count rigged to prevent him from taking office. President Calderón and the Mexican people had managed to avert a return to the chaos of the decade of revolution. Mexico has come far on the way to recovery from the years of revolutionary chaos. But Mexico's leaders and its people will have to continue their efforts to fulfill the promises made in the aftermath of the revolution.

Timeline

November 21, 1876	Porfirio Díaz becomes President of Mexico.
October 4, 1910	Díaz claims that he has won reelection as president.
November 20, 1910	Francisco I. Madero calls for a revolution with the Plan of San Luis Potosi. Francisco "Pancho" Villa seizes the city of Juárez, Mexico, from government forces in support of the Madero initiative.
1910	Emiliano Zapata forms the Liberation Army of the South to support Madero.
May 25, 1911	Francisco León de la Barra becomes interim president of Mexico.
June 1911	Zapata breaks with Madero because he feels he has betrayed the revolution by appointing conservative de la Barra.
November 6, 1911	Madero becomes president of Mexico.
November 25, 1911	Zapata issues the Plan of Ayala setting out a blueprint for agrarian reform.
February 18, 1913	Madero is deposed in a coup and then assassinated four days later. Victoriano Huerta is proclaimed president.

March 23, 1913	The Plan of Guadalupe is issued calling for revolt against Huerta.
June 1914	Pancho Villa and his army capture Zacatecas, an almost impregnable city in central Mexico, from Huerta's forces.
July 14, 1914	Huerta is forced to resign.
February 5, 1917	A new constitution is approved.
August 20, 1917	Venustiano Carranza becomes president under the new constitution.
1918	The Spanish influenza, killing millions worldwide, reaches epidemic levels in the war-torn areas of Mexico.
April 9, 1919	Emiliano Zapata, the revolutionary hero, is assassinated, probably at the direct order of Carranza.
May 21, 1920	Carranza is assassinated.
December 1, 1920	General Álvaro Obregón assumes the presidency after elections held under a temporary president.
December 1, 1924	Plutarcho Elías Calles becomes president after a normal electoral process.
1926–1929	The Cristero Rebellion against the suppression of the Catholic Church erupts.
December 1, 1934	Lázaro Cárdenas becomes president of Mexico.

March 18, 1938	President Cárdenas nationalizes the Mexican petroleum industry.
1994	The Zapatista Army of National Liberation tries to launch a new revolution but is stopped by federal troops.
July 2, 2000	Vicente Fox is elected president of Mexico, the first president to come from an independent political party since the Mexican Revolution.
December 1, 2006	Felipe Calderón takes office after a fiercely contested presidential election.

Glossary

agrarian: having to do with agriculture, in this case the distribution of land that is good for farming

conquistadores: the Spanish soldiers who captured Mexico for Spain in the 1500s

coup d'état: a violent change in government, often undertaken by the military to replace a sitting political leader

criollos: white descendants of the original Spanish settlers of Mexico

Cristeros: the "Christ fighters," supporters of the Catholic Church who fought in open rebellion against the Calles government between 1926 and 1929

ejido: communal farm originated by the Aztec that became popular after agrarian reform in the 1900s

hacendados: the small group of powerful landowners who controlled Mexico's haciendas

haciendas: the large plantations (farms) of pre-Revolutionary Mexico

indigenous peoples: the peoples who lived in the area of Mexico before the arrival of the Spanish; also called Amerindians

mestizos: people in Mexico with mixed Spanish and indigenous ancestry

peonage: the economic system under which poor agricultural workers in Mexico lived until the revolution

peons: agricultural workers on the haciendas

Porfiriato: the name used to refer to the rule of General Porfirio Díaz, which began in 1876 and ended with the revolution of 1910

Villistas: supporters of Pancho Villa

Zapatistas: supporters of Emiliano Zapata; they came from the southern region of Mexico and fought with him for land reform

Who's Who?

Doroteo Arango (1878–1923): Later known as Francisco "Pancho" Villa, Arango was born in Durango, Mexico. Arango was a peasant of little education. After his father's death, he worked as a sharecropper (tenant farmer) to support his mother. Various stories are told of how he became a revolutionary and whether he was actually just a bandit taking advantage of the uncertain times. He apparently spent his prerevolutionary years following in the footsteps of the man whose name he adopted, Francisco Villa. The original Villa was a famous bandit who was the "Robin Hood" of Mexico, stealing from the rich to give to the poor.

When Francisco Madero issued his Plan of San Luis Potosi, calling for active rebellion, "Pancho" Villa found a cause he could believe in. At the Battle of Juárez, Villa defeated the Mexican government troops and seized the city in November 1910. When Huerta forced Madero from office in a military coup, Villa took to the field again to force a return of control to the revolutionaries. Joining with Zapata in support of Venustiano Carranza, the cavalry troops in Villa's *División del norte* (Division of the North) became part of the Constitutionalist Army of Mexico. Villa was an able commander, good at recruiting men and ingenious at finding means of paying them through attacks on haciendas and train robberies.

Carranza saw Villa as a threat to the constitutional government and undermined his army in favor of one led by General Álvaro Obregón. Villa responded by trying to make himself the hero of the movement by defeating the government troops holding Zacatecas.

His victory led to the fall of Huerta but did not improve his relationship with Carranza. Villa and Zapata combined forces and denounced Carranza, temporarily costing him the presidency. When he was later expelled from Mexico City by a victorious Carranza, Villa attempted to overthrow him.

Since Carranza had firm support from the United States, Villa attacked the city of Columbus, New Mexico, on March 9, 1916. U.S. president Woodrow Wilson responded with an expedition to capture Villa. Neither the American expedition nor the government forces were able to find Villa, who had gone into hiding. In 1920 he reached an accommodation with the Mexican government and retired from active life. On July 23, 1923, he was assassinated. He remains a colorful figure in Mexican history and the subject of much mythology.

Plutarcho Elías Calles (1877–1945): Calles was born in Sonora. He came from a prominent family but suffered much hardship as a child. A schoolteacher, he was attracted to the ideas of Francisco Madero and became active in the revolutionary movement. In 1915 he was named governor of the state of Sonora and in 1919 was named secretary of commerce, industry, and labor by President Carranza. This was a very important role under the new constitution. Calles supported Obregón when he broke with Carranza and joined Obregón's government after he became president.

Elected president in 1924, Calles began the process of secularizing Mexico by enacting the Calles Law, which resulted in a three-year revolt among Catholic supporters known as the Cristeros. Calles willingly stepped aside so that Obregón could be elected for a second term in 1928. After Obregón was assassinated, historians felt that Calles became de facto president, controlling the actions of the next three presidents to serve in the office, while serving them as minister of war. In 1934, he selected Lázaro Cárdenas as the next president, only to find that Cárdenas was stronger than expected and chose to rule by himself. Calles was later arrested and deported by Cárdenas for interfering with the government. He was allowed to return to Mexico in 1941 and died there in 1945.

Venustiano Carranza (1859–1920): Carranza was born in 1859 in Cuarto Ciénegas. His father had been in the Mexican army under Benito Juárez and had retired to raise cattle. He was able to obtain a good education and was interested in government service from the beginning of his career, serving in various local, state, and national positions. Carranza was an early supporter of Francisco Madero, and when Madero assumed the presidency, Carranza was named minister of war.

After Huerta deposed Madero and assumed the powers of a dictator, Carranza issued the Plan of Guadalupe, which called for a revolt by the Mexican states against the federal government. After months of fighting, Huerta was removed from office. Infighting among the revolutionary leaders followed, and a series of interim presidents ruled the country, including Carranza himself beginning in 1915. In September 1916, Carranza convened an assembly to revise the 1857 constitution. Instead, an entirely new constitution was written to incorporate the revolutionary demands.

Carranza was elected to the presidency under the new constitution. He served out his presidency and then tried to select his own successor so that he could rule through him. When Carranza's old ally Álvaro Obregón was elected instead, Carranza tried to overthrow him by military force but was unable to do so. In May 1920, he was assassinated.

Porfirio Díaz (1830–1915): Born in Oaxaca, Díaz was a mestizo, claiming descent from Spanish conquerors and the indigenous Mixtec peoples. He joined the Mexican army and rapidly gained fame for his services there, becoming a brigadier general by 1861. In 1875, Díaz started a rebellion against the existing government of Mexico, and in 1876 he declared himself president. A firm believer that presidents should not be eligible for reelection, he stepped aside in 1880 for four years and watched the government disintegrate without his leadership. Welcomed back as president in 1884, he remained in power until 1910.

Díaz faced a weak Mexico with serious economic problems. He sought to move Mexico into the modern age by reforming the land distribution laws and encouraging foreign investment in the country to develop much needed transportation and communication networks. He considered himself to be a liberal and to have the greater good of the country as his focus. However, his methods for forcing Mexico into the modern world created great inequity in the country and led to the Revolution that began in 1910. Removed from office in 1911 as the Revolution began, Díaz left the country and moved to Paris, France, where he died in 1915.

Victoriano Huerta (1854–1916): Huerta was born in Colotlán to a mestizo father and an indigenous mother. An excellent student, he was able to escape his impoverished background because of his academic ability. While still young, he met an army general who was impressed with both his ability and his ambition, and who arranged for him to attend the Military College of Chapultepec, where he studied engineering.

Huerta advanced rapidly in the army. His military skills led President Madero to call on him to suppress revolts. However, he plotted with Madero's enemies to overthrow him in a military coup that divided the army and resulted in *La Decena Trágica*, the Ten Tragic Days of fighting among military units in Mexico City. Huerta deposed Madero, appointed a temporary leader, and then assumed power himself in February 1913. Huerta ruled as a military dictator, earning himself the nickname *El Chacal*, the Jackal. The combination of his policies and the opposition to his rule by the U.S. government led to his removal from office in July 1914.

Huerta left the country and traveled to several countries while attempting to raise an army to retake Mexico. While in the United States in 1916, he was confined to house arrest to deter his plotting against the Mexican government. He died in El Paso, Texas, on January 13, 1916, from cirrhosis of the liver.

Francisco León de la Barra (1863–1939): León de la Barra was born in 1863 in Querétaro and trained as a lawyer. A successful diplomat during the Porfiriato, he was ambassador to the United States when the revolution began and later served as foreign secretary in the final months of the Porfiriato. When Díaz resigned on May 25, 1911, León de la Barra was asked to serve as interim president until a president could be elected. He served less than six months, until Francisco Madero was elected and assumed office.

León de la Barra served again as foreign secretary during the Huerta presidency but then resigned and moved to Europe. He gained international fame as president of the Hague Tribunal, an international organization set up in the Netherlands in 1899 to help resolve disputes between countries. He was considered an expert on international law, and his services were called upon often in the years after World War I. He died in France in 1939.

Francisco I. Madero (1873–1913): Madero was born to one of the richest families in Coahuila. His family was of direct Spanish descent and wealthy enough that they could afford to have him educated in the United States and France. Madero felt that the Porfiriato was pushing the population so strongly toward modernization that it might incite a revolution and destroy the country. He put himself forward as an alternative to Díaz in the 1910 elections. His candidacy got him arrested and jailed for inciting a revolution. Escaping from prison, he fled to the United States after the government declared Díaz the winner of the election.

From the United States, Madero issued the Plan of San Luis Potosi, in which he claimed that the election was fraudulent and called upon the Mexican people to revolt. The resulting uprising led to the resignation of Díaz in 1911. Madero appointed León de la Barra as interim president until he could be legally elected to the office. Because León de la Barra was conservative, Madero's former allies took this as a sign that he would betray the revolutionary cause. After assuming the presidency, Madero did not immediately push through the agenda of the revolutionary leaders. His hesitation in this area led to further uprisings. Madero chose General Victoriano Huerta to lead the armies. Instead, Huerta plotted to overthrow Madero's presidency. The coup d'état was successful, and Madero was forced to resign on February 21, 1913. He was assassinated several days later. Authorities claimed that he was killed while trying to escape.

Álvaro Obregón: (1880–1928): Obregón was born in Sonora. A planter who became involved in local politics, Obregón supported Madero in the overthrow of the Porfiriato. He later helped Carranza gain power in the years after the overthrow of Huerta, serving as a military leader for him. Although a friend of Carranza, he broke with him when Carranza tried to prolong his stay in power by handpicking his successor.

Obregón led a successful military revolt against Carranza and his allies. After interim president Adolfo de la Huerta served until elections could be held, Obregón was elected to the presidency of Mexico in 1920. As president, Obregón worked to implement the reforms mandated by the new constitution. He is considered to be the first president to serve after the official end of the revolution. Obregón served his first term, and then his friend Plutarcho Calles was elected as his successor. He ran again for president in the 1928 election and was successful. As he returned to Mexico City to prepare to assume power, he was assassinated on July 17, 1928, by José de Léon Toral, a man studying to become a Roman Catholic priest who was angered by the suppression of the Catholic Church.

Emiliano Zapata (1879–1919): Zapata was born in Morelos. Zapata's father was independent and not subject to the peonage system but also not particularly wealthy. Zapata himself spoke an indigenous language and from the beginning was sympathetic to the Nahua community living in Morelos. He is remembered as the hero of the Revolution, even though he is one of the few figures who never became president. From the very beginning of the revolutionary period, he had a plan in mind for the redistribution of land to the peasants.

It was only natural, then, that he supported Madero against the Porfiriato. He served as the leader of the Liberation Army of the South that was formed to oppose Díaz. Zapata was very disappointed when each new president failed to move quickly to initiate agrarian reform. He produced the Plan of Ayala, calling for immediate agrarian reform and civil unrest as needed to achieve it. His supporters, the Zapatistas, rallied around the cry of *Tierra y Libertad*, which means "land and liberty." With the overthrow of Madero, all of the revolutionaries had a common enemy in his successor, Victoriano Huerta. The armies of Zapata in the south and Villa in the north united to bring Carranza to power. Zapata angered Carranza by keeping his army mobilized (armed), and Carranza eventually decided that he was a threat to the government and offered a bounty for his capture. Zapata was invited to a meeting by someone who claimed to be a revolutionary. Upon arrival at the meeting place on April 9, 1919, he was assassinated.

Source Notes

p. 8   James Creelman, "Porfirio Diaz," originally published in *Pearson's Magazine*, 1908, <www.historicaltextarchive.com/print.php?artid-138> (accessed July 7, 2007).

p. 8   Ibid.

p. 10   *New York Times*, "Cold-Blooded Assassination," February 24, 1913, 3.

p. 13   Marjorie Becker, *Setting the Virgin on Fire* (Berkeley: University of California Press, 1995), 20–21.

p. 15–16   Frank Tannenbaum, *The Mexican Agrarian Revolution* (Washington, DC: Brookings Institution, 1929), 12.

p. 16   Ibid., 12.

p. 16   Ibid., 13.

p. 17   Ibid., 14.

p. 17   P. Edward Haley, *Revolution and Intervention: The Diplomacy of Taft and Wilson with Mexico, 1910–1917* (Cambridge: MIT Press, 1970), 11.

p. 18   Michael J. Gonzales, *Mexican Revolution, 1910–1940* (Albuquerque: University of New Mexico Press, 2002), 263.

p. 20   Quoted in *New York Times*, "Obregon for Order as He Takes Office," December 1, 1920, 3.

p. 20   Matthew A. Redinger, *American Catholics and the Mexican Revolution 1924–1936* (Notre Dame, IN: University of Notre Dame Press, 2005), 3.

p. 23   Ivor Thord-Gray, *Gringo Rebel* (Coral Gables: University of Miami Press, 1960), 452.

p. 23   Ibid.

p. 24   Robert E. Quirk, *The Mexican Revolution and the Catholic Church 1910–1929* (Bloomington: Indiana University Press, 1973), 9.

p. 24   Edith O'Shaughnessy, *A Diplomat's Wife in Mexico* (New York: Harper & Brothers, 1916), 88.

p. 25   Gary MacEoin, *The People's Church* (New York: Crossroads, 1996), 44–45.

p. 25   Tomme Clark Call, *The Mexican Venture: From Political to Industrial Revolution in Mexico* (New York: Oxford University Press, 1953), 143.

p. 27   Haldeen Braddy, *Pershing's Mission in Mexico* (El Paso: Texas Western Press, 1966), 2.

p. 27   Robert Woodmansee Herr, *American Family in the Mexican Revolution* (Wilmington, DE: Scholarly Resources, 1999), 5.

p. 28   Ibid., 164.

p. 28   Anita Brenner, *The Wind That Swept Mexico* (Austin: University of Texas Press, 1943), 10–11.

p. 29   Robert E. Quirk, *The Mexican Revolution, 1914–1915: The Convention of Aquascalientes* (Bloomington: Indiana University Press, 1960), 1.

p. 29   Haley, *Revolution and Intervention*, 12.

p. 29   Herr, *American Family in the Mexican Revolution*, xii.

p. 29   Quirk, *Mexican Revolution 1914–1915*, 2.

p. 34   *Internet Modern History Sourcebook*, "Francisco Madero: The Plan of San Luis Potosi, November 20, 1910," <http://www.fordham.edu/halsall/mod/1910potosi.html> (accessed July 18, 2007).

p. 36   Peter V. N. Henderson, *In the Absence of Don Porfirio: Francisco León de la Barra and the Mexican Revolution* (Wilmington, DE: SR Books, 2000), 235.

p. 36   Quoted in Edward Marshall, "General Madero Talks of the Mexican Revolution," *New York Times*, May 14, 1911, Sunday Magazine, p. 1.

p. 37   Quoted in Edward Marshall, "General Madero Talks of the Mexican Revolution," *New York Times*, May 14, 1911, Sunday Magazine, p. 1.

p. 37   Henderson, *In the Absence of Don Porfirio*, xi.

p. 38   Thord-Gray, *Gringo Rebel*, 455.

p. 38   Rosa Mary Stoops, "Madero, Francisco I," <http://historicaltextarchive.com/sectionsphp?op=viewarticle&artid=145> (accessed July 17, 2007).

p. 39   Tannenbaum, *The Mexican Agrarian Revolution*, 160.

p. 40   O'Shaughnessy, *A Diplomat's Wife in Mexico*, 58–59.

p. 40–41   O'Shaughnessy, *A Diplomat's Wife in Mexico*, 58–59.

p. 41   Quoted in *New York Times*, "Huerta Disclaims Ambi-
             tion," February 19, 1913, 2.

p. 42   Quoted in *New York Times*, "Huerta Arraigns Wilson,"
             July 16, 1914, 2.

p. 42   Howard F. Cline, "Mexico: A Matured Latin American
             Revolution, 1910–1960," in *Is the Mexican Revolution
             Dead?* ed. Stanley R. Ross, (Philadelphia: Temple Uni-
             versity Press, 1966), 62

p. 44   John S. D. Eisenhower, *Intervention! The United States
             and the Mexican Revolution 1913–1917* (New York: W.
             W. Norton 1993), xvii.

p. 44   Quoted in Neil B. Carmony and David E. Brown, eds.,
             *Tough Times in Rough Places: Personal Narratives of Ad-
             venture, Death, and Survival on the Western Frontier* (Salt
             Lake City: University of Utah Press, 2001), 284.

p. 49   E. V. Niemeyer Jr., *Revolution at Querétaro: The Mexican
             Constitutional Convention of 1916–1917* (Austin: Univer-
             sity of Texas Press, 1974), 222.

p. 49   E. V. Niemeyer Jr., "Anticlericalism in the Mexican Con-
             stitutional Convention of 1916–1917," *The Americas*,
             11, no. 1 (July 1954): 31.

p. 49–50   Quoted in *New York Times*, "Protests to Mexico over Constitution," January 26, 1917, 10.

p. 50   Niemeyer, *Revolution*, 215.

p. 51   Larry D. Hill, *Emissaries to a Revolution* (Baton Rouge: Louisiana State University Press, 1973), 363–364.

p. 56   Quoted in *New York Times*, "The Mexican Constitution," February 26, 1917, 7.

p. 57   James D. Cockcroft, *Intellectual Precursors of the Mexican Revolution 1900–1913* (Austin: University of Texas Press, 1968), 234.

p. 59   Quoted in *New York Times*, "Carranza Refuses to Resign Office," May 7, 1920, 1.

p. 60   Charles C. Cumberland, *Mexican Revolution: The Constitutionalist Years* (Austin: University of Texas Press, 1972), 415.

p. 61   Quoted in *New York Times*, "Obregon for Order as He Takes Office," 3.

p. 61   Robert McCaa, *Missing Millions: The Human Cost of the Mexican Revolution* (Minneapolis: University of Minnesota Population Center, 2001), <www.hist.umn.edu/~rmccaa/missmill/mxrev.htm> (accessed December 10, 2006).

p. 61   Oscar J. Martínez, *Fragments of the Mexican Revolution: Personal Accounts from the Border* (Albuquerque: University of New Mexico Press, 1983), 214.

p. 61–62   Adolfo Gilly, *Mexican Revolution* (London: Verso, 1983), 330–331.

p. 62   Donald Hodges and Ross Gandy, *Mexico 1910–1982: Reform or Revolution?* (London: Zed, 1983), 45.

p. 65   Robert P. Millon, *Zapata: The Ideology of a Peasant Revolutionary* (New York: International Publishers, 1969), 127.

p. 65   Tannenbaum, *The Mexican Agrarian Revolution*, 232.

p. 67   William Weber Johnson, *Heroic Mexico: The Narrative History of a Twentieth Century Revolution* (New York: Harcourt, Brace, Jovanovich, 1984), 386.

p. 70   John Lear, *Workers, Neighbors, and Citizens: The Revolution in Mexico City* (Lincoln: University of Nebraska Press, 2001), 341.

p. 70   Ibid., 342.

p. 70   Quoted in *New York Times*, "Obregon for Order as He Takes Office," 3.

p. 72   Michael Joseph McGuinness, "The Landscape of Labor Law Enforcement in North America: An Examination of Mexico's Labor Regulatory Policy and Practice," BNET.com, Spring 1998, 3, <http://findarticles.com/p/articles/mi_qa3791/is_199804/ai_n8796670> (accessed October 15, 2007).

p. 74   Jean A. Meyer, *The Cristero Rebellion: The Mexican People between Church and State 1926–1929* (Cambridge: Cambridge University Press, 1976), 13–14.

p. 76   Ibid., 211.

p. 78   Quoted in Oscar J. Martínez, *Fragments of the Mexican Revolution: Personal Accounts from the Border* (Albuquerque: University of New Mexico Press, 1983), 242.

p. 80   *New York Times*, "100,000 Mexicans Kneel at Shrine in Thanks for Peace," June 24, 1929, 1.

p. 80   Quoted in Redinger, *American Catholics and the Mexican Revolution 1924–1936*, 10.

p. 82   Adrian A. Bantjes, "Saints, Sinners, and State Formation: Local Religion and Cultural Revolution in Mexico," in *The Eagle and the Virgin: Nation and Cultural Revolution in Mexico, 1920–1940*, ed. Mary Kay Vaughan and Stephen E. Lewis, (Durham, NC: Duke University Press, 2006), 152.

p. 83   Quirk, *The Mexican Revolution and the Catholic Church 1910–1929*, 9.

p. 84   Quoted in Stephen Bonsal, "Mexico's Main Need," *New York Times*, July 17, 1921, 80.

p. 84   Call, *The Mexican Venture*, 144.

p. 84   Luis A. Marentes, *Jose Vasconcelos and the Writing of the Mexican Revolution* (New York: Twayne, 2000), 128.

p. 86   Ibid.

p. 86   Irene V. O'Malley, *The Myth of the Revolution* (New York: Greenwood, 1986), 3.

p. 86   Quoted in Stephen Bonsal, "Mexico's Main Need," *New York Times*, July 17, 1921, 80.

p. 88   Edith O'Shaughnessy, *Diplomatic Days* (New York: Harper & Brothers, 1917), 30.

p. 89   Edwin Lieuwen, *Mexican Militarism: The Political Rise and Fall of the Revolutionary Army 1910–1940* (Albuquerque: University of New Mexico Press, 1968), xi.

p. 90   Hodges and Gandy, *Mexico 1910–1976*, 29.

p. 90   Thord-Gray, *Gringo Rebel*, 458.

p. 92   Hodges and Gandy, *Mexico 1910–1976*, 32.

p. 93–94   Cumberland, *Mexican Revolution: The Constitutionalist Years*, 415.

p. 94   Herr, *American Family in the Mexican Revolution*, 243.

p. 94   Linda B. Hall and Don M. Coerver, *Revolution on the Border: The United States and Mexico, 1910–1920* (Albuquerque: University of New Mexico Press, 1988), 159.

p. 96   Robert Freeman Smith, "The United States and the Revolution, 1921–1950," in *Myths, Misdeeds and Misunderstandings: The Roots of Conflict in U.S.-Mexican Relations*, ed. Jaime E. Rodríguez O. and Kathryn Vincent (Wilmington, DE: SR Books, 1997), 191.

p. 99   Millon, *Zapata*, 128–129.

p. 99   Call, *The Mexican Venture*, 79.

p. 102   Alexandra Fuller, "Mexico's Pilgrim Cowboys," *National Geographic* 212, no. 2, August 2007, 139.

p. 103   Quoted in Manuel Roig-Franzia, "In Mexico, the Car-
              dinal and the 'Crazies,'" *Washington Post*, August 28,
              2006, A8.

p. 105   H. James McLaughlin, "Schooling in Mexico: A Brief
              Guide for U.S. Educators," ERIC Digest, <www.eric
              digests.org/2003-4/mexico.htmlChapter 8> (accessed
              January 10, 2007).

p. 105–106   Frank Bohn, "Mexico under the New Regime: Dr.
              Vasconcelos and Educational Regeneration," *New York
              Times,* February 12, 1921, 11.

p. 106   Michael C. Meyer, "Introduction," *Essays on the Mexi-
              can Revolution: Revisionist Views of the Leaders*, ed.
              George Wolfskill and Douglas W. Richmond (Austin:
              University of Texas Press, 1979), xvii.

p. 107   Octavio Paz, "Mexico and the United States: Positions
              and Counterpositions," in *Mexico Today*, ed. Tommie
              Sue Montgomery (Philadelphia: Institute for the Study
              of Human Issues, 1982), 18.

p. 107   Alan Knight, *Mexican Revolution* (New York: Cam-
              bridge University Press, 1986), 1:2.

p. 107   Daniel Levy and Gabriel Székely, *Mexico: Paradoxes of
              Stability and Change* (Boulder, CO: Westview, 1983),
              34.

p. 114–115   Quoted in James C. McKinley Jr., "Election Ruling in Mexico Goes to Conservative," *New York Times*, September 6, 2006, <www.nytimes.com> (accessed September 6, 2006).

p. 115   Cline, "Mexico: A Matured Latin American Revolution, 1910–1960," 65.

p. 115–116   Susan Kaufman Purcell, ed., *Mexico in Transition: Implications for U.S. Policy* (New York: Council on Foreign Relations, 1988), 3.

p. 117   Daniel Levy, *Mexico: Paradoxes of Stability and Change*, 2nd ed. (Boulder, CO: Westview, 1987), 32.

p. 119   Howard Handelman, *Mexican Politics: The Dynamics of Change* (New York: St. Martin's, 1997), 11.

Bibliography

Babington, Charles. "New Congress Unlikely to Rush Toughest Issues." *Washington Post*, November 27, 2006.

Baldwin, Deborah. *Protestants and the Mexican Revolution: Missionaries, Ministers and Social Change*. Urbana: University of Illinois Press, 1990.

Becker, Marjorie. *Setting the Virgin on Fire*. Berkeley: University of California Press, 1995.

Braddy, Haldeen. *The Paradox of Pancho Villa*. El Paso: Texas Western Press, 1978.

———. *Pershing's Mission in Mexico*. El Paso: Texas Western Press, 1966.

Brenner, Anita. *The Wind That Swept Mexico*. Austin: University of Texas Press, 1943.

Call, Tomme Clark. *The Mexican Venture: From Political to Industrial Revolution in Mexico*. New York: Oxford University Press, 1953.

Carmony, Neil B., and David E. Brown, eds. *Tough Times in Rough Places: Personal Narratives of Adventure, Death, and Survival on the Western Frontier*. Salt Lake City: University of Utah Press, 2001.

Cline, Howard F. *Mexico: Revolution to Evolution 1940–1960*. London: Oxford University Press, 1962.

Cockcroft, James D. *Intellectual Precursors of the Mexican Revolution 1900–1913.* Austin: University of Texas Press, 1968.

Cumberland, Charles C. *Mexican Revolution: The Constitutionalist Years.* Austin: University of Texas Press, 1972.

———. *Mexican Revolution: Genesis under Madero.* Austin: University of Texas Press, 1952.

Eisenhower, John S. D. *Intervention! The United States and the Mexican Revolution 1913–1917.* New York: W.W. Norton, 1993.

Gilly, Adolfo. *Mexican Revolution.* London: Verso Editions, 1983.

Gonzales, Michael J. *Mexican Revolution, 1910–1940.* Albuquerque: New Mexico Press, 2002.

Haley, P. Edward. *Revolution and Intervention: The Diplomacy of Taft and Wilson with Mexico, 1910–1917.* Cambridge: MIT Press, 1970.

Hall, Linda B., and Don M. Coerver. *Revolution on the Border: The United States and Mexico, 1910–1920.* Albuquerque: University of New Mexico Press, 1988.

Handelman, Howard. *Mexican Politics: The Dynamics of Change.* New York: St. Martin's, 1997.

Henderson, Peter V. N. *Félix Díaz, the Porfirians, and the Mexican Revolution.* Lincoln: University of Nebraska Press, 1981.

———. *In the Absence of Don Porfirio: Francisco León de la Barra and the Mexican Revolution.* Wilmington, DE: SR Books, 2000.

Herr, Robert Woodmansee. *American Family in the Mexican Revolution.* Wilmington, DE: Scholarly Resources, 1999.

Hill, Larry D. *Emissaries to a Revolution*. Baton Rouge: Louisiana State University Press, 1973.

Hodges, Donald, and Ross Gandy. *Mexico 1910–1976: Reform or Revolution?* London: Zed, 1979.

———. *Mexico 1910–1982: Reform or Revolution?* London: Zed, 1983.

Johnson, William Weber. *Heroic Mexico: The Narrative History of a Twentieth Century Revolution*. New York: Harcourt, Brace, Jovanovich, 1984.

Lear, John. *Workers, Neighbors, and Citizens: The Revolution in Mexico City*. Lincoln: University of Nebraska Press, 2001.

Levy, Daniel. *Mexico: Paradoxes of Stability and Change*. 2nd ed. Boulder, CO: Westview, 1987.

Levy, Daniel, and Gabriel Székely. *Mexico: Paradoxes of Stability and Change*. Boulder, CO: Westview, 1983.

Lieuwen, Edwin. *Mexican Militarism: The Political Rise and Fall of the Revolutionary Army 1910–1940*. Albuquerque: University of New Mexico Press, 1968.

MacEoin, Gary. *The People's Church*. New York: Crossroads, 1996.

Marentes, Luis A. *Jose Vasconcelos and the Writing of the Mexican Revolution*. New York: Twayne, 2000.

Martínez, Oscar J. *Fragments of the Mexican Revolution: Personal Accounts from the Border*. Albuquerque: University of New Mexico Press, 1983.

McCaa, Robert. *Missing Millions: The Human Cost of the Mexican Revolution*. Minneapolis: University of Minnesota Population Center, 2001. <www.hist.umn.edu/~rmccaa/missmill/mxrev.htm>.

McKinley, James C., Jr. "Election Ruling in Mexico Goes to Conservative." *New York Times*, September 6, 2006. <www.nytimes.com>.

McLaughlin, H. James. "Schooling in Mexico: A Brief Guide for U.S. Educators." ERIC Digest. <www.ericdigests.org/2003-4/mexico.htmlChapter 8>.

Meyer, Jean A. *The Cristero Rebellion: The Mexican People between Church and State 1926–1929*. Cambridge: Cambridge University Press, 1976.

Millon, Robert P. *Zapata: The Ideology of a Peasant Revolutionary*. New York: International Publishers, 1969.

Montgomery, Tommie Sue, ed. *Mexico Today*. Philadelphia: Institute for the Study of Human Issues, 1982.

Niemeyer, E. V., Jr. "Anticlericalism in the Mexican Constitutional Convention of 1916–1917." *The Americas* 11, no. 1, July 1954.

———. *Revolution at Querétaro: The Mexican Constitional Convention of 1916–1917*. Austin: University of Texas Press, 1974.

O'Malley, Irene V. *The Myth of the Revolution*. New York: Greenwood, 1986.

O'Shaughnessy, Edith. *Diplomatic Days*. New York: Harper & Brothers, 1917.

———. *A Diplomat's Wife in Mexico*. New York: Harper & Brothers, 1916.

Presley, James. "Mexican Views on Rural Education, 1900–1910." *The Americas* 20, no. 1, July 1963.

Purcell, Susan Kaufman, ed. *Mexico in Transition: Implications for U.S. Policy*. New York: Council on Foreign Relations, 1988.

Quirk, Robert E. *The Mexican Revolution and the Catholic Church 1910–1929*. Bloomington: Indiana University Press, 1973.

———. *The Mexican Revolution, 1914–1915: The Convention of Aquascalientes*. Bloomington: Indiana University Press, 1960.

Redinger, Matthew A. *American Catholics and the Mexican Revolution 1924–1936*. Notre Dame, IN: University of Notre Dame Press, 2005.

Reed, John. *Insurgent Mexico*. New York: Greenwood, 1914.

Rodríguez O., Jaime E., and Kathryn Vincent, eds. *Myths, Misdeeds and Misunderstandings: The Roots of Conflict in U.S.-Mexican Relations*. Wilmington, DE: SR Books, 1997.

Roig-Franzia, Manuel. "In Mexico, the Cardinal and the 'Crazies,'" *Washington Post*, August 28, 2006.

Ross, Stanley R. *Is the Mexican Revolution Dead?* Philadelphia: Temple University Press, 1966.

Scheina, Robert L. *Villa: Soldier of the Mexican Revolution*. Washington, DC: Brassey's, 2004.

Stoops, Rosa Mary. "Madero, Francisco I." <http://historical textarchive.com/sections.php?op=viewarticle&artid=145>.

Tannenbaum, Frank. *The Mexican Agrarian Revolution*. Washington, DC: Brookings Institution, 1929.

Thord-Gray, I[vor]. *Gringo Rebel*. Coral Gables, FL: University of Miami Press, 1960.

Tompkins, Frank. *Chasing Villa: The Story behind the Story of Pershing's Expedition into Mexico*. Harrisburg, PA: Military Service Publishing Company, 1934.

Vaughan, Mary Kay, and Stephen E. Lewis, eds. *The Eagle and the Virgin: Nation and Cultural Revolution in Mexico, 1920–1940.* Durham, NC: Duke University Press, 2006.

Wolfskill, George, and Douglas W. Richmond, eds. *Essays on the Mexican Revolution: Revisionist Views of the Leaders.* Austin: University of Texas Press, 1979.

For Further Reading and Websites

BOOKS

Brunk, Samuel. *The Posthumous Career of Emiliano Zapata: Myth, Memory, and Mexico's Twentieth Century.* Austin: University of Texas, 2008.

Hamilton, Janice. *Mexico in Pictures.* Minneapolis: Twenty-First Century Books, 2002.

Hinshaw, Kelly Campbell. *Art across the Ages: Ancient Mexico.* San Francisco: Chronicle Books, 2007.

Hunter, Amy N. *The History of Mexico.* Broomall, PA: Mason Crest, 2002.

Johnston, Tony. *The Ancestors Are Singing.* New York: Farrar, Straus and Giroux, 2003.

Katz, Friedrich. *The Face of Pancho Villa: A History in Photographs and Words.* El Paso, TX: Cinco Puntos, 2007.

Scheina, Robert L. *Villa: Soldier of the Mexican Revolution.* Dulles, VA: Potomac Books, 2005.

Serrano, Francisco. *The Poet King of Tezcoco: A Great Leader of Ancient Mexico.* Toronto: Groundwood Books, 2007.

WEBSITES

Central Intelligenge Agency: The World Factbook
<https://www.cia.gov/library/publications/the-world-factbook/geos/mx.html>

The Central Intelligence Agency's fact-book site for Mexico offers information on geography, population, government, economy, communication, and transportation.

Historical Text Archive
<http://historicaltextarchive.com/links.php?op=viewslink&sid=224>
The Historical Text Archive is an online site that collects articles (almost all are secondary sources) about the Mexican Revolution.

Library of Congress
<http://lcweb2.loc.gov/frd/cs/mxtoc.html>
The Library of Congress Country Study for Mexico provides information on geography, history, economy, culture, and other aspects of Mexican life.

Mexico Connect
<www.mexconnect.com>
This online magazine has information about Mexico, its history, and its culture.

Mexico for Kids
<http://www.elbalero.gob.mx/index_kids.html>
This site, maintained by the Mexican government, is intended for young users to introduce them to Mexican history and culture.

Visual Geography Series®
<http://www.vgsbooks.com>
Visit vgsbooks.com, the home page of the Visual Geography Series®, which is updated regularly. You can get linked to all sorts of useful online information, including geographical, historical, demographic, cultural, and economic websites. The vgsbooks.com site is a great resource for late-breaking news and statistics about a variety of nations, including Mexico.

Index

Agraristas, 77

Alamo, 45

Anti-Reelectionist Party, 34

Arango, Doroteo. *See* Villa, Pancho

armies: Colorados (Red Flaggers), 39; current national, 92–93; power of private, 89, 90–91; Villistas, 35, 36, 90; Zapatista Army of National Liberation, 116–117; Zapatistas, 35, 36, 42, 90

artists, 106

Aztecs, 26

Bantjes, Adrian A., 82

Becker, Marjorie, 13

Bonillas, Ignacio, 59

Braddy, Haldeen, 27

Brenner, Anita, 28

Calderón, Felipe, 103, 119–120

Call, Tomme Clark, 25, 84, 99

Calles, Plutarco Elías, 60, 66–67, 75–79, 86, 110

Camacho, Avila, 101

Cárdenas, Lázaro: attempted coup against, 92; and Catholic Church, 80; nationalization of foreign holdings, 94–96, 107–108

Carranza, Venustiano: assassinated, 60; and COM, 68, 69–70; and Constitution of 1917, 46–47, 49, 56–57, 59; coup attempted by, 112–113; and Obregón, 59–60; and U.S. intervention, 43–44

Casa del Obrero Mundial (COM), 68–70

Catholic Church: Catholic percent of population, 73; and Constitution of 1917, 51, 54, 73–76; and Cristero Rebellion, 76–80; and culture, 102;

easing of limits on, 101; and education, 20–22, 101; and indigenous peoples, 20, 22–23; and land ownership, 20, 23; and patron saint of Mexico, 77; and politics, 75, 102–103

Cedillo, Saturnine, 92

Chacal, El (Jackal), 42

citizenship, 21–22, 92

Ciudad Juárez, Treaty of, 37

civil war, 42–44

Cline, Howard F., 42, 115

Cockcroft, James D., 57

Colorados (Red Flaggers), 39

Columbus, New Mexico, 9, 44

communications network, 18, 28, 29

Constitution of 1824, 50

Constitution of 1857, 50

Constitution of 1917: and Catholic Church, 51, 54, 73–76; convention, 46–50; and culture, 82; and education, 54; enforcement of mandated changes, 56–57, 59, 113; and foreign investment, 49–50, 52–54, 57, 93–94; and

indigenous peoples, 51, 55–56; and land ownership, 50–52, 54, 55; and natural resources, 52–54; overview of, 51; and peasants, 51–52, 54–55; and workers, 54, 70

coups d'etat: attempted, 92, 112–113; government by, 25–26, 41, 89–90

cowboy pilgrimage, 102

Creelman, James, 7–8

Cristero Rebellion (Cristiada), 76–80

Cristo Rey (Christ the King) Monument, 102

culture: and Catholic Church, 102; and class system bias, 25; and Constitution of 1917, 82; of indigenous people, 56, 81; modern, 105–108; and national identity, 32, 56, 81–82, 85–86

Cumberland, Charles C., 60, 93–94

deaths, 61–62

Decena Trágica, Las, 40

de la Barre, Francisco León, 37

Díaz, José Maria Pino, 7

Díaz, Porfirio: and democracy, 12; and Madero, 32, 34; and modernization of land ownership system, 14–18; and U.S., 8. *See also* Porfiriato

economy: current status, 109, 116; development of middle class, 24; development of natural resources, 12; foreign investment, 18, 28–29; and NAFTA, 108; nationalization, 94–96, 107–108

education: and Catholic Church, 20–22, 101; and Constitution of 1917, 54; current status, 103–105; and indigenous peoples, 25, 82, 83–84, 105; secularized, 80–86. *See also* literacy

Eisenhower, John S. D., 44

ejidos, 66, 99

Federal Labor Act (1931), 72

foreign investment: benefits, 18, 27–29, 93; and Constitution of 1917, 49–50, 52–54, 57, 93–94; nationalized, 94–96, 107–108

Fox, Vincente, 110

Gandy, Ross, 62, 92

Gilly, Adolfo, 61–62

Gonzales, Michael J., 18

government: by coups d'etat, 25–26, 41, 89–90; by oligarchy, 92; political parties, 110; structure, 96; 2006 election, 117, 118, 119–120

hacendados, 12–14, 16–18, 23

Haley, P. Edward, 17, 29

Handelman, Howard, 119

Henderson, V. N., 36

Herr, Irving, 94

Herr, Robert Woodmansee, 27–28, 29

Hill, Larry D., 51

history, writing, 9

Hodges, Donald, 62, 92

Huerta, Victoriano, 7, 40–42, 68

Photo Acknowledgments

The images in this book are used with the permission of: Hulton Archive / Getty Images, 5 / © Corbis, 13, 17, 37, 76, 83 / © Michael Maslin Historic Photographs / Corbis, 15 / © Malcolm Lubliner / Corbis, 20 / © Bettmann / Corbis, 23, 46, 62, 67, 69, 77, 93, 111 / The Art Archive / National History Museum, Mexico City / Gianni Dagli Orti, 31, 36 / Hulton-Deutsch Collection / Corbis, 39, 89 / © Underwood & Underwood / Corbis, 41 / © Mary Evans Picture Library / The Image Works, 51 / © Albert Harlingue / Roger Viollet / The Image Works, 56 / © Alinari Archives / The Image Works, 65 / Associated Press, 79, 114, 117 / © Danny Lehman / Corbis, 98 / © Keith Dannemiller / Corbis, 102.

Front cover: © Time & Life Pictures / Getty Images

About the Author

Susan Provost Beller is the author of twenty-three history books for young readers. She is most fascinated with what motivates ordinary people to find it within themselves to do extraordinary things. She writes from her home in Charlotte, Vermont, when she is not traveling to see historic sites or visiting with her three children and five grandchildren. Her one wish is that someone would invent a time machine so she could go back in time and really see the past.